A Guide to Building

NATURAL SWIMMING POOLS

by

MICHAEL LITTLEWOOD

Schiffer Publishing Ltd

4880 Lower Valley Road • Atglen, PA 19310

Library of Congress Control Number: 2015954067

Designed by Andrew Crane
Cover design by Molly Shields
Type set in Tempus Sans ITC/NewsGoth Lt BT
ISBN: 978-0-7643-5083-2
Printed in China

Published by Schiffer Publishing, Ltd.
4880 Lower Valley Road
Atglen, PA 19310
Phone: (610) 593-1777; Fax: (610) 593-2002
E-mail: Info@schifferbooks.com
Web: www.schifferbooks.com

Other Schiffer Books by the Author:
Natural Swimming Pools: Inspiration for Harmony with Nature, ISBN: 978-0-7643-2183-2

Other Schiffer Books on Related Subjects:
Water Gardens and Natural Pools, ISBN: 978-0-7643-3367-5

For our complete selection of fine books on this and related subjects, please visit our website at www.schifferbooks.com. You may also write for a free catalog.

Schiffer Publishing's titles are available at special discounts for bulk purchases for sales promotions or premiums. Special editions, including personalized covers, corporate imprints, and excerpts, can be created in large quantities for special needs. For more information, contact the publisher.

We are always looking for people to write books on new and related subjects.
If you have an idea for a book, please contact us at proposals@schifferbooks.com.

CONTENTS

FOREWORD

At long last, natural swimming pools are becoming part of the British landscape. Their many advantages over sterile 'blue rectangle' chemical pools are now widely recognised. They enhance their surroundings, giving you a swimming pool that is also a wonderful water garden and landscape feature; all the materials used can be environmentally friendly; they provide a safe habitat for wildlife, including endangered species; they offer opportunities for nature watching and an educational resource for children; they save on water, energy, and maintenance; and they allow everyone to swim in chemical-free water in attractive surroundings.

The first natural pools were built in mainland Europe in the 1980s, and on the Continent the concept has come of age, with many thousands of private pools and hundreds of public and commercial ones. Acceptance of the idea in the UK has taken rather longer, but there are now hundreds of private pools and a number of British companies specialising in the installation of natural swimming pools. The first public natural pool has now opened in London; more are planned, and a number of commercial projects are in the pipeline.

When I first brought the concept of natural swimming pools to the UK in 2000, the task of publicising the wonderful attributes of the system proved almost impossible. It took numerous attempts to persuade even one publication to run an article on the subject. But within hours of its appearance the phone started ringing and did not stop for four days. The response was overwhelming.

With so many people requesting information I felt it was necessary to put it all together in a book. *Natural Swimming Pools: Inspiration for Harmony with Nature* was eventually published in 2005. This generated a new wave of enquiries from people across the world wanting information enabling them to build a pool themselves, or with the help of a builder. I therefore set about writing this book to provide a working manual that would allow anyone the enjoyment and satisfaction of building a natural pool.

The first edition, *Natural Swimming Pools: A Guide for Building*, was published in 2008, and this revised edition brings all of the technical information up to date and includes examples of more recent projects. I have consulted with many professional builders of natural swimming pools in the UK and Europe, and I am very grateful to them for providing me with so much technical assistance freely and willingly. While this may be a small industry, it has a big heart.

My first book should be considered for its inspiration, explanation, and information about natural pools and should be read before this manual, which aims to concentrate on construction and technical matters. As my first book is descriptive, I felt this manual should not only be more instructive, but should use a minimum of words and a maximum of illustrations in the form of photographs, drawings, and sketches. As the Chinese proverb says, 'One time seeing is worth a thousand times reading.'

This book should enable an experienced amateur builder or professional landscape gardener or builder to construct a natural swimming pool, and do so in the most efficient and economical way. As much information as possible has been included to assist you in undertaking the project, but it must be stressed that the descriptions of procedures and principles are necessarily generic and must be interpreted to accommodate your specific site requirements and conditions.

I hope you will be inspired to build your very own natural swimming pool.

Photo: Held-Teichsysteme GmbH

INTRODUCTION

This book contains 11 chapters. Chapter 1 is a brief overview of the overall building process with case studies. It also covers the design of the pool and the production of the drawings necessary for construction.

Chapter 2 covers the planning, preparation, and project management that need to be undertaken by the self-builder. Careful planning at this stage could save considerable time and money, as well as avoid many potential frustrations of the building process.

The actual building operations are described in Chapter 3 in the form of Notes and Action—a more 'user friendly' style of specifications. The material contained in the 'Conversions' section of this chapter in the first edition has now been expanded into a separate sixty-page book, *Natural Swimming Pools: Conventional Pool Conversion Guide*.

Chapters 4 and 5 cover the plumbing and electrical works, while chapter 6 describes the main structures that can be used with the pool, depending on your requirements and the overall design. Water is such an essential element in the natural pool system that it merits chapter 7 all to itself.

The planting of the regeneration zone is critical to the success of the whole system and chapter 8 covers this in detail.

Chapter 9 explains the ongoing care and maintenance required to keep your pool functioning well and looking good.

In chapter 10 I have included a number of construction details for the builder that are specific to a natural swimming pool. Other information that may prove useful can be obtained from my landscape detailing books.

Finally, in chapter 11, three glossaries are provided.

1

DEVELOPMENT

THE TASK

For the Self-Builder

No one can say that building a natural swimming pool is easy, but it is a uniquely satisfying and rewarding project for the self-builder. You are in complete control at every stage of the operation, and provided that you have confidence in your abilities, there is no reason why you should not be successful. You may well be a 'jack of all trades and master of none,' but this can be an advantage. You will be far more aware of the whole picture than a specialist or professional.

If you are reasonably fit and active then building your own natural swimming pool can be a very worthwhile and enjoyable challenge. Doing the job yourself will save you money and keep you fit, and— unlike when renovating a property—there is no pressure to complete by a certain deadline. In addition, you will have the satisfaction of doing something hugely beneficial for the environment and creating a wonderful amenity for yourself and your family.

Take ample time to think about how you will organise your project before you start work. The initial planning phase is the most important part of any project, especially when you are undertaking something for the first time, and time spent thinking now will be more than repaid in time, effort, and money saved later on.

Building a natural swimming pool is a major commitment, one that is difficult to cancel if you lose interest or discover it is too big a task. It is not always easy to find reliable contractors to take on partially completed work, especially if it is a DIY disaster. It is therefore essential to be honest with yourself from the outset.

Ask yourself: just how fit are you? How much time can you devote to the project? Are you fully aware of the total costs? Bear in mind the productivity of a self-builder is around half that of a skilled trade person. Remember that the longer the job takes, the more your enthusiasm may wane.

Work out your strengths and weaknesses at the outset and decide what you can and cannot do. Remember that you do not need to do all the work yourself; the project can be just as satisfying (and much less stressful) if you delegate those parts of the job in which you are less competent. Work out what help and support you can get from relatives and friends who may well have the skills you require and which contractors you will need to employ.

If you decide to use a contractor for any stage of the project, it is essential to ensure they are suitable, preferably from previous customers. Word of mouth is the best recommendation. Look out for contractors' signposts at sites you pass; no contractor will promote their services and invite inspection of their work if it is not up to standard.

Obtain more than one estimate. Invite contractors to see the site, discuss the project with them, and let them see the plans. Ask for a written estimate so when making comparisons there are no ambiguities. Check terms and conditions and warranties and confirm

timescales (both lead time and contract time), ensuring they will fit in with your programme. You should also check your feelings about working with any contractor. The price may be right, but their attitude may not be suitable for you.

If you utilise the help of friends and family, remember that organising unskilled labour is a job in itself. Try to identify mini-projects that can be completed within an afternoon, a day, or a weekend. This will allow people to feel a sense of achievement over a short period of time. Let them go away having had some fun and companionship, too.

If you call upon assistance when you need it, you will have the best of both worlds: the satisfaction of building your pool yourself and the reassurance of knowing that you have back-up when required. Paying for some professional help or advice is worthwhile and means you and your family and friends will be able to enjoy the fruits of your labour that much sooner.

Good luck!

OVERALL BUILDING PROCESS

The main aim of a natural pool is to provide clean natural water without the addition of any chemicals. This is achieved by a circulation system that operates automatically for a set period of time each day, thereby ensuring the natural filtration process is maintained. It is important to remember that it is not technology but biology that cleans a natural swimming pool.

Over the years, the natural pool system has been further developed by a number of companies, making it more sophisticated, although possibly some systems have become too complicated. A brief description of the systems developed by the major companies can be found in my first book.

The building process begins with site preparation. Setting out the design on the ground and ensuring that the levels are correct is the next task. The protection of existing features—especially trees—is essential. With trees, you need to ensure there will be no disturbance of the ground over the entire area of the tree canopy if at all possible.

This is followed by the excavation of the ground, ensuring that topsoil and subsoil are kept separate and that the profiles are correct. The ground is graded and compacted, and all sharp stones and other obstacles are removed. If necessary, a layer of sharp sand is spread over the base.

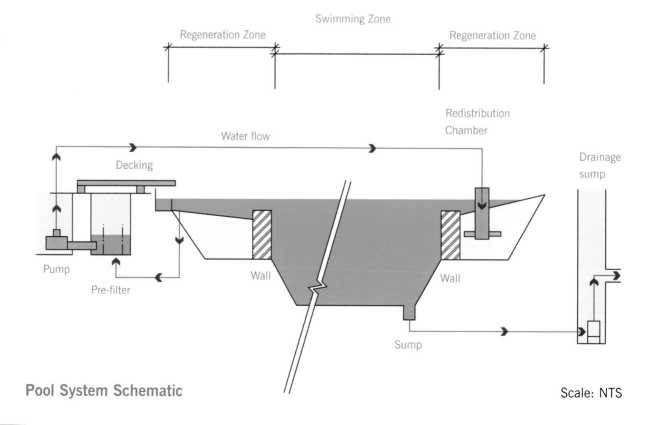

Pool System Schematic   Scale: NTS

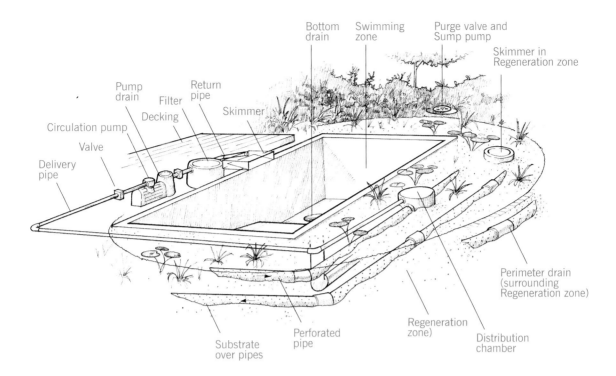

Bottom drain   Swimming zone   Purge valve and Sump pump

Skimmer in Regeneration zone

Pump drain   Return pipe

Filter

Decking   Skimmer

Circulation pump

Valve

Delivery pipe

Perimeter drain (surrounding Regeneration zone)

Substrate over pipes   Perforated pipe   Regeneration zone)   Distribution chamber

Natural Swimming Pool System Layout

Checks need to be made on the ground drainage and if necessary, a system installed to ensure that no water remains underneath the pool liner that could cause any upward pressure. Provision for an outlet drain from the bottom of the swimming zone at its deepest point should be included.

The underliner (geotextile) can then be laid over both the swimming and regeneration zones. This is easily cut and joined together with tape. On steep sloping sides it may be necessary to pin the material in place. The main liner (rubber) is then laid over the underliner. Where it has been cut to shape the pieces are then welded together. It is very important to ensure that neither liner has any contact with the surrounding soil at the edge of the pool. An edging appropriate for the site should be selected.

A curtain drain then needs to be installed around the edge of the pool to remove any surplus surface water run-off. This ensures that the pool water does not become contaminated.

The walls that separate the swimming and regeneration zones are built next. Decisions regarding the type of material and the height of the walls will have been made at the design stage. Some walls can be the full depth of the pool and others half-depth; some can be covered with the liners and others exposed—particularly if they are made of natural stone—to reveal their beauty. A small perimeter wall is necessary to hold both liners in place.

After the main construction has been completed, the plumbing and electrical works follow. First the pump chamber is built under a deck or located nearby in its own house—either above or below ground—containing the pump and all the controls, valves, etc. From here the basic pipework is laid to the regeneration zone and on to the skimmers before returning to the pump to complete its cycle. Other elements requiring plumbing connections, such as waterfalls, streams, and bubble jets are also undertaken at this stage. Mains electrical supply to the pump will be necessary and a transformer for low-voltage lights will need to be installed in the pump chamber/house.

After this, the structural features surrounding the pool can be built. The main structural elements that need to be considered are decks, jetties, boardwalks,

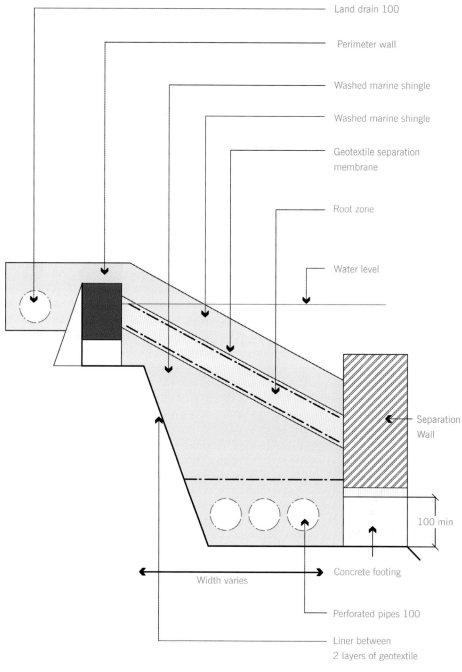

Land drain 100

Perimeter wall

Washed marine shingle

Washed marine shingle

Geotextile separation membrane

Root zone

Water level

Separation Wall

100 min

Concrete footing

Width varies

Perforated pipes 100

Liner between 2 layers of geotextile

Regeneration Zone Schematic

Scale: NTS

bridges, ladders, and steps. Their construction is usually of timber.

Finally, the gravel substrate is placed in the regeneration zone, after which the pool can be filled with water and planted. Water and plants are at the heart of the natural swimming pool system and both

need to be given very careful attention. The water used for filling the pool must be carefully tested. Plants need to be clean and free of any soil.

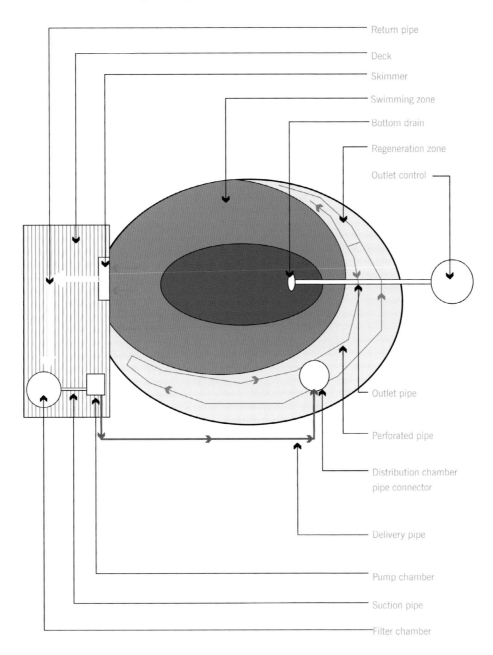

Return pipe
Deck
Skimmer
Swimming zone
Bottom drain
Regeneration zone
Outlet control
Outlet pipe
Perforated pipe
Distribution chamber pipe connector
Delivery pipe
Pump chamber
Suction pipe
Filter chamber

Water Flow Schematic

Scale: NTS

PROCESS EXAMPLES

1. ROB MUYLWYK WHARTON, ONTARIO, CANADA

Rob decided to build his own pool after reading about natural swimming pools in my book *Inspiration for Harmony with Nature*.

He had intended to install a conventional chemical pool and was on the verge of signing the contract when he stumbled upon a newspaper article about natural pools. He writes, 'Clearly this type of pool/pond would eliminate all our reservations about the pool we had planned: significantly less energy use, no chemicals, and a solution congruent with our natural environment, both in and out of the swimming season. After doing our research it was clear that we needed the natural swimming pools books written by UK NSP guru Michael Littlewood, his earlier *Inspiration for*

Harmony with Nature and his more recent *A Guide for Building*. The first book certainly lived up to its title, as it gave us many ideas for our project, as well as thorough background information. The *Guide for Building* became our Bible as we gradually worked out the design parameters and preliminary specifications for our pool-to-be.

'We found a friendly local landscape contractor very eager to get into the NSP business, and after we taught him everything we had learned so far he gave us a nice proposal with an even nicer price, well over our budget. At this point we couldn't possibly go back to a chemical pool and we couldn't afford to have an NSP built, so there was just one way out, the DIY route.'

Marking out the swimming area

Placing the
skimmer

Installing the
underliner

Unrolling the
1600 lb liner,
showing the
'rolled holder'

Rob spent the following winter filling
a notebook with design sketches and
working out how he could do the job with
the tools and budget available to him.
'Again I relied heavily on Littlewood's
books, in addition to internet resources,'
he says. He then commissioned a local
landscape architect, Karen Bannister, to
provide all the necessary designs and
working drawings.

In June 2011 he started construction,
hiring an excavator with an operator to
dig and shape the hole. From this point
onward he did the entire job himself,
with one exception: 'we needed the help
of all the friends and neighbours that we
could rustle up in order to get the 1600lb
(725kg/114 stone) rubber liner rolled out
and spread out.' He built a 'rolled holder'
for the liner that proved very helpful.

Unfolding and
draping the liner
and working in
the folds

First water – to
keep the ground
water down

Building the wall

Rob's pool comprises a main and overflow pond with a total volume of 136,000 litres (30,000 gallons) and a surface area of 130sq m (1400sq ft). The swimming area is 13m 70cm by 3m 5cm (45 by 10ft), or 48sq m (520sq ft). It has a depth of 1m 10cm (3ft 8in) at the shallow end, rising to 2m 35cm (7ft 8in) at the deep end. In the regeneration zone, which has a surface area of 50sq m (556sq ft), the water depth is 5cm (2in), sloping to 35cm (14in) at the wall.

The liner is geotextile laid under a synthetic rubber 45mil EDPM liner, and also in the regeneration zone under the substrate. The walls are constructed of western red cedar timber on a concrete footing. The deck is made of local white cedar to match the existing decks in the garden, and the steps to the pool are made of western red cedar. The substrate is 38 to 76mm (1½ to 3in) Haydite (river rock) topped with pea gravel. The placement of the substrate proved to be a very large job. Because Rob put the walls inside the lined area more substrate than usual was required.

The plumbing consists of a bottom drain, a perimeter drain, and 5cm (2in) diameter perforated filter pipes under the substrate. Two Aquascape SK-900 skimmers were installed, and a 55-gallon barrel biofilter was installed between the skimmer and the pump house. The pump is a 4200 gph type in a pump chamber 61cm (2ft) in diameter and 91cm (3ft) high. It takes one and a half hours for the total volume to flow through the pump.

The photographs show the work at various stages. The project took somewhere between six and nine months, which was intermittent, subject to time available and the weather. Apart from the initial excavation, the 'liner party', and twenty minutes' help from a neighbour, Rob did all the work himself. In early August 2013, he completed the planting, filled the pool with water, and took his first swim.

'This was quite a large DIY project,' says Rob. 'I could never have pulled this off without the books of Michael Littlewood and his considerable technical assistance.' He and I exchanged many emails during the construction process in which I helped him with site-specific technical queries.

Thanks to Rob Muylwyk and his family for supplying this information and giving permission for it to be included here.

2. JAMES AND MARY ATHERTON

James and Mary Atherton built their own natural swimming pool at their new home in the Blackdown Hills in Somerset. They had bought the property—on 0.6 hectares (1.5 acres) of sloping ground—in spring 2006. The idea to create a pool initially came about because they were undertaking improvements to the house, demolishing the dilapidated flat roof extension and replacing it with extensions with conventional roof tiles. Building regulations stipulated a need to create a clear route for the rainwater collected from the roof to follow. They directed this to a ditch at the edge of their field, but realised that they could also use it to create a pond *en route*.

They then came across an article about natural swimming pools. Writing about their project in the winter 2009 issue of *Green Building*, they say, 'What we found really attractive were the photographs of the delightful environment, with lush

planting of water lilies and two boys sitting on a deck swishing their feet in the water. We were hooked! The idea that you could create a natural play space for children and adults that blended in superbly with the garden and was great for wildlife seemed too good to be true!

'We searched the Internet for more information until we came across Michael Littlewood, who is a landscape designer and a renowned authority on natural swimming pools. We bought his book, *Natural Swimming Pools: A Guide for Building* and found it invaluable and inspirational. It has information about design, construction, maintenance, and planting. It is an essential guide to consult before considering embarking on such a scheme.'

By this time they had already started making their pond. It was only 1m (3ft 3in) deep, and they quickly realised

that for the pond to become a natural swimming pool it would need to be deeper. This made the whole job more difficult and necessitated some rebuilding of retaining walls that were damaged as they attempted to deepen the pond with a digger.

They discovered they would need to create drainage channels below the pool, feeding into a soakaway, to prevent groundwater accumulating beneath the liner. Rather than dig trenches by hand, they employed a subcontractor to do the job of digging trenches and fitting drainage pipes.

The retaining walls, which were made with concrete blocks, had to be covered by an underliner to protect the 1mm thick Greenseal rubber liner. They say, '[We were] shocked by its weight. It took six of us to slowly move it into position. It was, in the end, a very tidy large-scale 'tailoring' job. We had an enormous rectangular tank surrounded by a gentle oval shape. This made a complex three-dimensional form and we didn't want lots of wrinkles or bulky folds. The team did a fantastic job.'

Finally, the pool was filled with water. They capped the retaining wall separating the swimming and regeneration zones with a wooden plate topped with

hamstone offcuts from a local quarry that hold the wooden plate down and provide an attractive finish. The 5m by 3m (16ft 5in by 9ft 10in) deck area, which is constructed from recycled timber, overhangs the swimming area and incorporates a sturdy ladder to help swimmers climb from the pool. The spacious deck area means there is room for a table and chairs and still enough space to sunbathe.

The gravel they intended to use for the substrate turned out to be full of dirt and debris, so they sourced four tonnes of washed pebbles from the Internet. They addressed initial problems with algae with the purchase of a Green Genie 48000

filter and an Oase Aquamax Eco 16000 pump. The pump sits on the floor of the swimming area and pumps water to the Genie on the edge of the planting zone. They housed this 40cm (16in) above the pool so it creates some turbulence when the water hits the surface to help with oxygenation.

The Athertons say their pool has been a great hit with the whole family. 'The combined area of deck and pond provide a terrific location for relaxing and making the most of the view.' It was a focal point for their son's 21st birthday party and their grandchildren have derived much pleasure from it, even taking the dinghy out for a sail.

'We are delighted with the pool we have created, but with hindsight I should have read Michael's guide first, as this would have saved me a lot of time, trouble, and money! I should have made the pool 50cm (20in) deeper and about 3m (9ft 10in) longer. The extra size would make diving safe and have given us more room to swim. But despite the hard work and mistakes, we have a remarkable 'plunge' pool that will provide pleasure for us for many years to come.'

Thanks to James and Mary Atherton for supplying this information and allowing me to include their project here.

DESIGN

Before you can proceed you will need to have a design produced for your pool and garden. It is most important that all drawings are accurate and to scale.

Planning and Design have been described in considerable detail in my book *Natural Swimming Pools*, so they will not be repeated here. As a reminder, the following steps are given as a basic process for creating a detailed design from which all the construction drawings can be produced:

1. **Survey Plan**

2. **Property Base Plan**

3. **Site Inventory Plan**

4. **Site Analysis Plan**

5. **Requirements**

6. **Functional Plan**

7. **Conceptual Plan**

8. **Alternative Designs**

9. **Final Design**

The task is not difficult and can be quite enjoyable, but it does take time, which you may not care to assign to it.

The assistance of a professional landscape architect or garden designer could prove most beneficial and save you time and money. If possible use one who has experience with the natural swimming pool system.

Considerations

In addition to the notes given in my previous book, consider the following in the design of your pool and surroundings.

Slopes

Excavation can cause land to move and endanger the stability of nearby houses. As a pool introduces large areas of water, it must not create the danger of flooding for the properties below yours. This means that the pool basin has to be sunk into the ground; otherwise extensive measures are necessary to create a supporting wall. Always seek professional advice.

The sloping plot will need to have differences in height plotted on the site survey plan. The easiest method for this is to use graduated measurements with a spirit level: anything higher than the starting point is marked +, anything below is marked -.

Size

The size of the pool is the most important decision. The size of the garden and how much of it is to be devoted to the pool are crucial aspects, but the pool should be as large as possible. The minimum surface area for a pool is 40 square metres; it is possible to have smaller pools, but more filtration will be necessary. Most garden pools are from 70-250 metres, including the regeneration (vegetation) zone. The latter should be about the same size as the swimming area. If it can be larger then so much the better. The more frequently it is used, the larger it needs to be.

Swimming area size

The area depends on the requirement of the users.

As a guide value for the swimming area, it is recommended for it to be at least 8.0 × 4.0m. This is calculated from 4 × 1.5m strokes + 2.0m for a stretched out body length. If a round pool is chosen, a minimum diameter of 5.0m is recommended.

Deep and shallow water

A depth of 1.25 to 1.50 metres is enough for swimming (less if you only want to bathe and not swim), but a 2 to 2.5 metre depth makes swimming more pleasant. Deeper water means the water quality is better. There is also less light penetration and reflection, resulting in less algae. The water will take longer to warm up, but it will not encourage the growth of algae.

Shape

Nature produces irregular, not geometric shapes. If you have the space, you could have gently curving edges to your pool, which after a few years will look completely natural.

The smaller the pool, the more regular the outline of the pool needs to be. It doesn't have to be square or rectangular—it could be circular or oval. However, the areas around the swimming zone can be square and geometric in shape and this can make the construction of the supporting walls easier and cheaper. There will be less hand welding.

Access

Access to the swimming zone can be gentle, such as walking in from a beach area, diving in from a deck or jetty, or both.

To be able to wade in, a gentle slope of 1:3 or 1:4 will be required, meaning you would reach a depth of one metre when you are 3 or 4 metres from the shore or the bank. Beware that if the slope becomes steeper the swimmer must take greater care, as the liner can be slippery. Steps may be considered or even a ladder.

Ensure that a "leaping off" deck or jetty hangs over deep water!

Temperature

The maximum temperature for the effectiveness of the natural system depends upon the country and location. It is 28-30°C for the UK and northern Europe.

Site location

Warm water for bathing and plant growth is required—especially in the United Kingdom—but not too much or it will encourage algae growth. Having part of the planting zone in the shade for a few hours in summer can prove beneficial. Late morning till mid-afternoon is best; and then the shallower areas won't warm up too quickly and there will be enough exchange of cooler water with warmer water from the lower layer. The larger the pool the slower the warming process, but the water will retain its heat on the cooler days for longer and later in the season.

Regeneration zone

While the regeneration zone needs a certain width, it does not have to enclose the pool. The pool edge can remain clear at the spot you intend to enter the pool, or where children might want to play. To compensate, the planting area can take up more room where overflow water drains away, for example.

The Surrounds

If the pool is not near your existing terrace or patio then an area for gathering, sunbathing, relaxation, etc., will be essential. The surfacing could be hard, such as stone or timber, or soft, such as a lawn or even bark chippings, depending upon the intensity of use and its location. Hard materials retain heat more than grass or vegetation. This area will also require protection from adverse climatic elements, especially wind. Any surplus soil from the excavation could be used to form banks or mounds that can be made into pleasing shapes and sizes. These can trap the sun but never cause a buildup of heat.

Trees and shrubs planted on the mounds will provide protection from the wind. If there is insufficient room for ground modelling use raised beds and hedges or shrubs.

Requirements

You may find the included checklist helpful and useful.

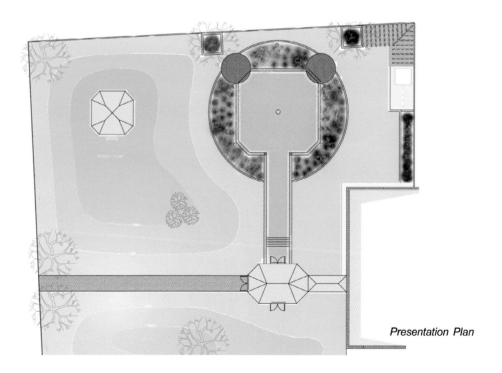

Presentation Plan

CHECKLIST FOR BUILDING
Questions to ask

Main use of the Pool

Swimming laps/length
Casual exercise/play

Diving board
Beach
Children's play pool

Design Factors

NUMBER AND SIZE
One pool with surrounding aquatic plants
Two pools - one for swimming and one for plants.
Size (50% required for plants to clean water)

DEPTH
Shallow 1.2 – 1.4m
Deep 2.0 – 2.4m.
Deep to 2.0 – 2.8m
Diving 3.0 – 4.0m

Solar heating
Solar power
Colour of liner

ACCESS/ENTRY
Ladder
Steps
Beach
Shallow shelf

STYLE
Naturalistic
Formal   geometric   symmetrical
Contemporary
Other

LIGHTING
Pool lighting   Paving and garden lighting   Fibre optics
Low voltage systems.
Lights from the house   or outbuildings to pool

Surfacing

USES
Sunbathing

Entertaining

MATERIALS
Consistent with building/garden
Comfortable for bare feet
Stone   Brick   Tile   Wood   Concrete   Pre-cast concrete blocks
Interlocking block units
Edges/Trim type   Colour

Enclosure

VISUAL
Around property   just pool
Style preferred

PRACTICAL
Fence/Wall   Height   Type   Materials
Gates   Materials   Size   Type

Features

Waterfalls
Streams
Fountain – In pool   Outside pool   In garden

Structures

Pool house for changing
Gazebo   Arbour   Pergola   Bridge
Sculpture – In pool   Outside pool
Storage shed

Survey Plan

A detailed topographic survey plan of the property will have been produced for the design stage, but if not one is necessary.

It could save you considerable time and trouble if the plan is undertaken by a professional surveyor; you should obtain an estimate first.

If you wish to do it yourself, the following notes may be useful.

Survey the part of the garden or landscape where the pool is to be. For this you will need a ruler, measuring tape, a spirit level, and pegs for marking out the spots. They can be made from roof battens sawn into 30-50 cm pieces and sharpened to a point at one end.

You will need a few reference points, such as the corner of the house, a fence post, or border stone from which you can measure the garden elements. The simplest method is triangulation. If there is a tree in the garden, then measure it from three fixed points. Once you have noted these measurements you have a fixed point for the tree, which can be entered at the right point on your ground plan of the garden. In this way you can establish the key features of your garden. If these features are more complicated, the right angle method is better. A right-angled triangle has the proportions 3:4:5, which has been converted into the practical measurements 60: 80: 100 cm, so the right angle forms the basis for the measurement.

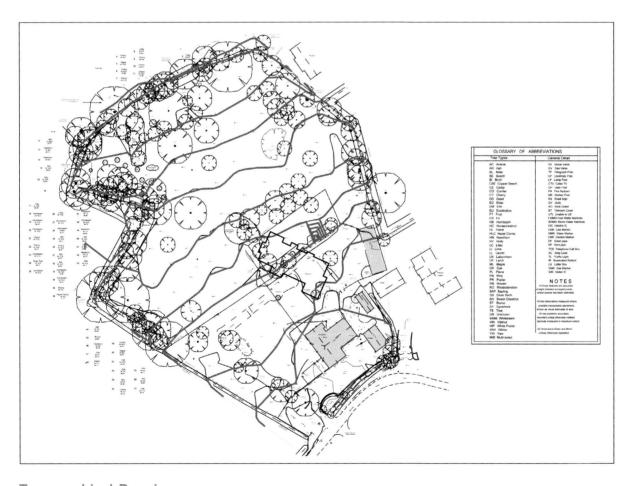

Topographical Drawing

Professionals use devices such as prisms, but you can make a right angle from 2 roof battens 60 and 80 cm long with the ends 100 cm apart. This angle can then be placed on a reference point. Key features can be used as reference points, or string can be stretched across the area and become the reference point. One end is 0 and the measure is placed along the reference line, a right angle is formed to the right or left, and measurements are taken. Don't rush this and carry out 2 or 3 checks, as mistakes cause more work and add more time to the project.

All the points in the garden can be measured using a ranging line, a measuring tape, and a right angle of 60: 80: 100.

You can hire a laser level and take readings at measured peg points. Leave the pegs in the ground and show them on your survey plan. Setting out and excavation is then easy using a laser level, but measure again.

WORKING DRAWINGS

Once you are fully satisfied with your design—whether it is for the whole garden or the pool—it is necessary to have working drawings prepared. Again, these can be produced by yourself or a professional. Examples are shown. These working drawings usually consist of the following:

Site Plan – This should show access for vehicles and equipment, such as excavators, dump trucks, etc.; the location for spoil and soil heaps; and the storage of plants and machinery, and any materials required for the project.

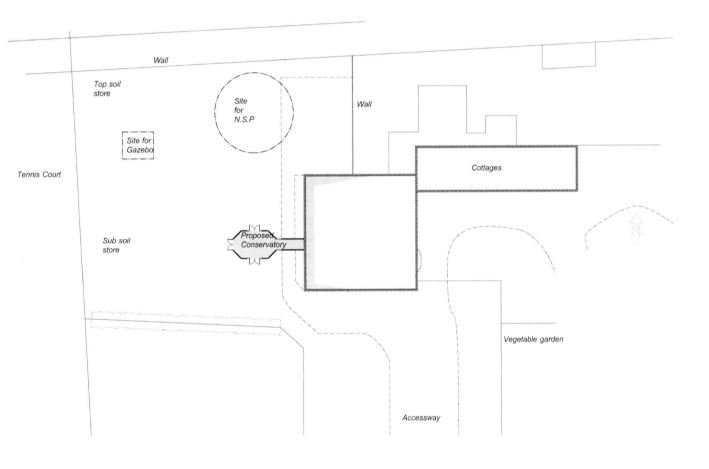

Site Plan

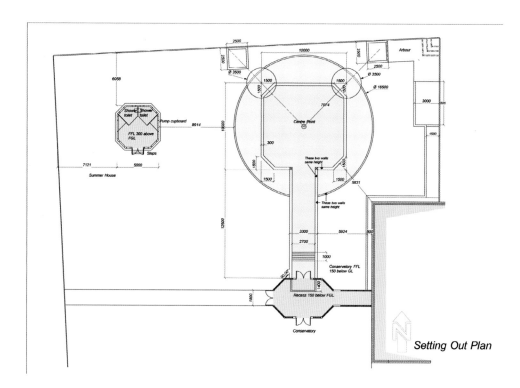

Setting Out Plan

Layout Plan – This should show all the dimensions of all the proposed enclosures, structures, surfacing, planting, etc.

Grading/Levels Plan – This is based on the site survey plan and should show the existing and proposed levels for all buildings, driveways, paths, steps, walls, and all other ground areas.

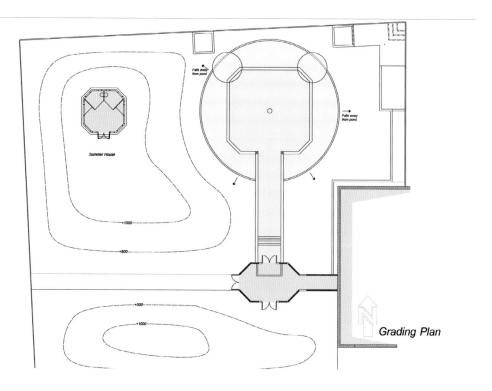

Grading Plan

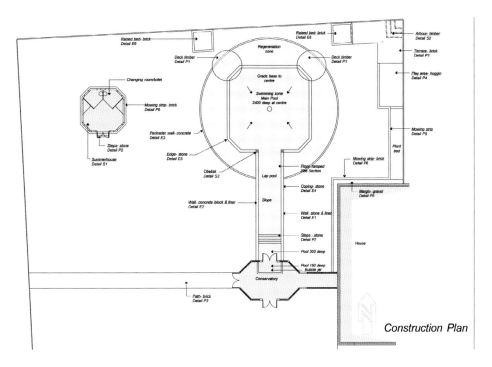

Construction Plan

Construction Plan – This drawing should provide a key for all the individual elements of the project, linking them to the construction details. These are usually shown separately as section and elevation drawings.

Planting Plan – This should locate and identify all items of plant material to be used and any existing plants retained or removed. A plant list, including quantities, sizes, and varieties should appear on this drawing or on a separate list.

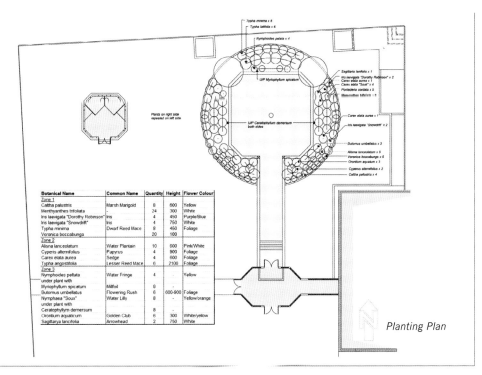

Botanical Name	Common Name	Quantity	Height	Flower Colour
Zone 1				
Caltha palustris	Marsh Marigold	8	600	Yellow
Menthyanthes trifoliata		24	300	White
Iris laevigata "Dorothy Robinson"	Iris	4	450	Purple/Blue
Iris laevigata "Snowdrift"	Iris	4	750	White
Typha minima	Dwarf Reed Mace	8	450	Foliage
Veronica beccabunga		20	100	
Zone 2				
Alisna lanceolatum	Water Plantain	10	600	Pink/White
Cyperis alternifolius	Papyrus	4	900	Foliage
Carex elata aurea	Sedge	4	600	Foliage
Typha angostifolia	Lesser Reed Mace	6	2100	Foliage
Zone 3				
Nymphoides peltata	Water Fringe	4		Yellow
under plant with				
Myriophyllum spicatum	Milfoil	8	-	
Butomus umbellatus	Flowering Rush	6	600-900	Foliage
Nymphaea "Soux"	Water Lilly	8	-	Yellow/orange
under plant with				
Ceratophyllym demersum		8		
Orontium aquaticum	Golden Club	6	300	White/yellow
Sagittarya lancifolia	Arrowhead	2	750	White

Planting Plan

SERVICES

Note

Before constructing a new pool you must consider the location of all underground and overhead utilities/services. All these need to be recorded on a drawing, either on the site survey plan or on a separate one—the services plan.

Electric/Telephone

Usually located at your electric meter, connected to the power company outlet. Electric/phone lines are installed together in the same trench if underground, located a minimum of 600mm (24in) below ground. For exact location contact your utility company, which will locate these underground lines or have the site scanned.

Gas

Located at the gas meter and installed toward the front of the home. Gas pipes probably run through the rear of a property. Once all the utilities are located, consider any underground water systems.

Water supply

Locate the main water supply to the property and ensure that you make a connection for a supply to the pool. In some very old properties check that any underground pipes are not made of lead.

Septic tank

The exact location of septic lines and tank must be pinpointed. Consult the local health department or contact the septic installer for septic site plans. Locate your pool 10m from septic tanks and lines.

IMPORTANT: Check drains with local council for all building regulation requirements. Septic tanks and wells should never be moved because of the high cost, unless the old system needs replacing.

Wells

Wells should be a minimum of 5m from the pool. Check with the local environment agency.

House foundation drains/land drains

Original building site plans should be examined to locate any underground water systems, such as foul, surface, and roof. Make sure you install any drainpipes away from the pool area to avoid problems later.

Flood zones

It would be advantageous to check with the environment agency (in the UK) or local planning authority if your proposed pool is on a flood plain or zone.

These should be shown on the services plan, along with any proposed services.

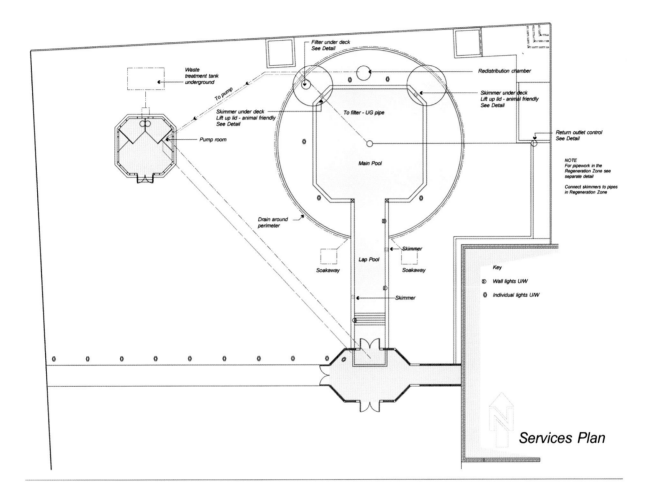

Filter under deck
See Detail

Waste
treatment tank
underground

To pump

Redistribution chamber

Skimmer under deck
Lift up lid - animal friendly
See Detail

Skimmer under deck
Lift up lid - animal friendly
See Detail

To filter - UG pipe

Return outlet control
See Detail

NOTE
For pipework in the
Regeneration Zone see
separate detail

Connect skimmers to pipes
in Regeneration Zone

Pump room

Main Pool

Drain around
perimeter

Skimmer

Lap Pool

Soakaway

Soakaway

Key

⊗   Wall lights U/W

✹   Individual lights U/W

Skimmer

N

Services Plan

MEASUREMENTS & CALCULATIONS

The builder should find this information helpful for measuring quantities, etc.

Note - The various formulae for calculating volumes will give measurements in cubic feet or metres.

It is necessary for the pool builder to know the dimensions of the pool—including the surface area and the volume of water—for use when ordering materials.

Regular shapes - Squares, rectangles, circles, and triangles present the least difficulty in calculating their dimensions.

Squares and rectangles - Calculate dimensions in metres or in decimal fractions of feet (e.g., 1.5 ft for 18 in). Multiply the length (l) of the pond by the width (w) to obtain the surface area. Multiply this figure by the depth (d) of the pool to establish its volume.

Circular shapes - Square the radius of the pool (v × v) and multiply this by the mathematical constant pi (3.14) to obtain the surface area. To calculate the volume, multiply this figure by the depth (d).

Irregular shapes - For simple shapes use the maximum length and width to calculate the surface area and for the volume calculate the length, width, and depth as for a regular shape. Complex informal shapes can be

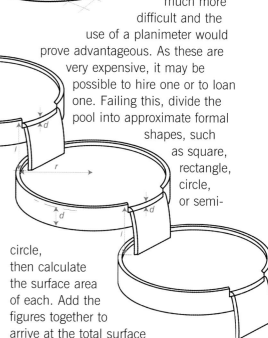

much more difficult and the use of a planimeter would prove advantageous. As these are very expensive, it may be possible to hire one or to loan one. Failing this, divide the pool into approximate formal shapes, such as square, rectangle, circle, or semi-circle, then calculate the surface area of each. Add the figures together to arrive at the total surface area. To obtain the volume, multiply the above figure by the overall depth of the pool.

Using computer aided design will make scaling and calculating volumes and areas much easier.

Calculations

When you have completed all your drawings, the measurements have to be transferred to the ground. Using a method based on right angles, every important point of the pool outline can be measured at a right angle measured from a selected fixed point of reference. Simple mathematical formulae enable calculation of the earth masses to be excavated.

Volume

The volume of your pool (gallons or litres) should be worked out roughly—even at this stage—for the sake of a few budgetary calculations. If you are going to have a waterfall, fountain, or filter, then you will need a pump. The volume of your pool will be an essential guide to the amount of water the pump will be required to circulate and also what size filtration unit will be necessary.

The formula is:

gallons = length × breadth × depth × 6.25 (all in feet)

litres = length × breadth × depth × 1,000 (all in metres).

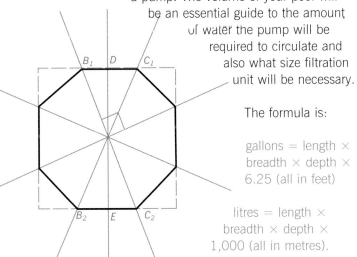

Marking out an octagon

Mark out a square the length and width of the pond as described on page 38. Set a peg in the centre of the square. Multiply the width of the pond (D-E) by .4142 to determine the length of the straight sides. B-C are positioned centrally on and at right angles to D-E. Mark out the axis lines (B1-C2 and B2-C1) and use a right angle at the centre to mark the remaining corners of the octagon.

Marking out an ellipse

You can do this with two stout poles and a loop of strong twine. Set the poles firmly

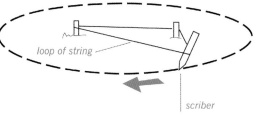

loop of string

scriber

in the ground. The distance between them and the length of the loop will determine the finished shape. The closer the poles are together, the squatter the ellipse will be. Place the loop of twine over the poles and pull it taut with a scriber. Drag the scriber while keeping the twine taut around the pole to mark out the elliptical shape on the ground. The scriber can be a liquid soap bottle filled with diluted emulsion paint or a strong sharp object that scores the ground.

Scaling up a freeform shape

Even though it has a freeform shape, an informal pond can be easily scaled up from a plan and marked out on the ground. This is done by stretching out a central line (using string or measuring tape) on the ground taken from two fixed points, such as a tree and the corner of a garden shed. To translate the shape on to the ground, mark off regular measurements along this line at 30cm (1ft) or 1m (3ft) intervals, depending on the size of the pond. From these equal points mark off in each direction—at right angles from the line—the distance to the outside edge of the pond, then use a loop of rope or hosepipe to form the final shape of the pond.

Level rims

Establish a datum point corresponding to the finished rim of the pond and use the following method to ensure perfect levels.

Straightening and spirit level

After the topsoil has been removed, tap the datum peg into the ground about 1m (3ft) outside the perimeter of the pond. Map the whole contour of the pond out with pegs. Use the straightedge and spirit level to check that the top of each peg is level with the top of the datum peg.

Source: *The Water Garden*, Anthony Archer-Wills

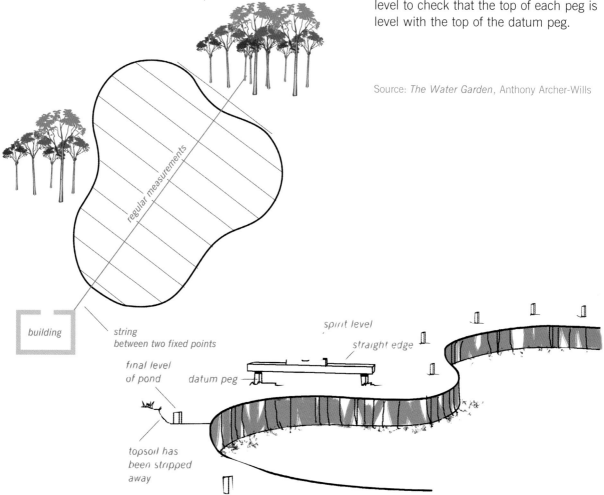

building

string
between two fixed points

regular measurements

spirit level

straight edge

final level
of pond   datum peg

topsoil has
been stripped
away

Photo: Oase

Photo: Will Woodhouse – Woodhouse Natural Pools Ltd

2

MANAGEMENT

PROJECT PLANNING

Having produced all the necessary drawings, now is the time to consider the project in detail.

To ensure that your project is completed entirely to your satisfaction, it is necessary to plan the entire operation with meticulous care and attention to every detail.

You will need to know what work you can undertake with confidence and what work will need to be done by other people who have far more experience. Costs and time will also determine the scope of work.

The first task is to think about the timescale. How long do you want to work on the project? When do you want it completed? How much manpower can you get to help you?

It is a large project, and it is worth considering using various people with appropriate skills.

For example, it is better to hire the man with his excavator than you just hiring the machine. He will do a much better job and be far quicker. Likewise, if you have walls to build, a skilled block layer can also take less time and be more economical in the long run. Again, it depends on time and money. If the block wall is going to be completely covered by a liner then the work can be done by you with help from unskilled workers.

Welding the liner is not a job to be undertaken by just anyone, as it is a skilled operation. The cost of the liner is far too expensive for mistakes, especially if leaks are made. Having the liner on site is advantageous because it is cut precisely for the existing layout and produces hardly any folds.

You could make use of the services offered by well-known manufacturers and have the liner tailor made, produced in one piece in the factory and sealed with a full guarantee.

Other tasks, such as filling the regeneration zone with substrate and water, along with the planting, can be carried out by the builder. If sufficiently experienced with plumbing then the fittings, pumps, skimmers, etc., could also be added. All the electrical work must be undertaken by a qualified electrician, which is a legal requirement in the UK and possibly elsewhere.

Do ensure you buy good quality plants and remember aquatics grow quickly, so it is not essential to buy large specimens.

Planting may look easy, but the need for a planting plan and schedule should not be overlooked. The plan should consider all aesthetic visual and functional aspects.

Planning the project should consider all the various components, operations, trades, etc.

Looking at the sequence of operations is a good starting point - as follows:

SEQUENCE OF OPERATIONS

There are a number of basic operations that have to be undertaken for the construction of a natural swimming pond, such as:

Strip topsoil and save for re-use

Excavate ground by machine and remove sub-soil from site

Regrade subsoil where necessary

Trim pool to shape by hand

Lay underliner

Lay top liner

Construct retaining walls using material selected

Build outer drain

Build inner drainage system

Build pump chamber

Install pump

Construct recirculation pipework

Install skimmers and filters

Place substrate in position

Build deck, steps, ladder, etc. (swimming zone)

Plant regeneration zone

Fill with water

Test whole system

With careful planning, the construction process can be undertaken with a minimum of difficulty. However, construction can result in environmental damage, especially erosion, siltation, and soil compaction. Measures to protect soil,

Photo: Stefan Lehnert – Bioteich

water, and plants should be taken before construction begins.

Planning Schedule

Producing a bar chart helps you realise the time required to undertake each operation and can also indicate where outside assistance is required. This is especially useful when hiring machinery and equipment—with or without operators.

Consult the example given to make your own "bar chart." Make allowances for inclement weather.

BAR CHART

Details	Week												
	1	2	3	4	5	6	7	8	9	10	11	12	13
Survey site	●												
Setting out		●											
Strip top soil and stockpile		●											
Excavate ground		●											
Remove sub-soil from site (if necessary)		●											
Trim pool shape by hand			●										
Install underground drainage			●										
Lay underliner				●									
Lay top liner				●									
Construct retaining walls					●	●							
Build outer drainage						●							
Build inner drainage system						●							
Build pump chamber							●						
Undertake electrical work								●					
Construct recirculation system									●				
Install skimmers and filters										●			
Build deck, steps/ladder (swimming zone)											●		
Place substrate in position												●	
Plant regeneration zone												●	
Fill pool with water													●
Test whole system													●

MATERIALS

Make a list of all the materials required (see example below) for the project. Contact companies and suppliers for costs and delivery time, and when you have finally made your choice add the information to your list. Be sure to have everything confirmed, as telephone orders are not always recorded.

Materials requirement list

Item		Quantity	Cost	Supplier	Delivery Date
SERVICES/UTILITIES	Electrical supply/				
	Water supply				
GROUNDWORKS	Sand				
	Hardcore				
DRAINAGE	Pipes				
	Soakaway				
WALLS	Concrete				
	Stone				
	Timber				
	Others				
LINING	Underliner				
	Liner				
PLUMBING	Perforated pipes 100 dia				
	Pipes 50 dia				
	Flange pipe				
	Suction hose				
	Filters				
	Filter chambers				
	Skimmers				
	Pump chambers				
	Pump				
SUBSTRATE	Gravel 10-30mm				
	Gravel 5-20				
ELECTRICAL	Pump connections				
	Lights				
	Heating				
PLANTING	Plants				
WATER	Supply to fill pool				
FINISHING	Deck steps, ladder				
	Jetty, bridge				

EQUIPMENT & MACHINERY

Large equipment and machinery are usually hired, but if you are using a specialist contractor he will have his own, leaving you free of this undertaking.

Ensure bookings are made to coincide with your programme. Obtain costs and check against your budget.

Photo: Fairwater Ltd – Bionova

BILL OF QUANTITIES

Having obtained all the information for materials and equipment, it is very useful to complete a "bill of quantities" for the whole project, ensuring that nothing has been overlooked.

Bill of Quantities

Description	Quantity	Unit	Cost: Labour & Sub-contractors	Materials	Total
Drawings Detailed technical drawings					
Setting-Out Set out pool and other preliminary works					
Groundworks Strip topsoil, pool area, and mound on site for re-use if possible Strip subsoil and prepare spoil area Excavate pool, carting spoil to on-site location Regrade spoil site, replace topsoil, and leave machine graded, ready for final preparation					
Drainage Underliner drainage to accommodate ground water Drainage sump to accept below liner drainage and outlet Install 160mm pipe to floor of pond and terminate in drainage sump.					
Walls Pour ring footing for wall Separation wall					
Perimeter Secure liners behind perimeter wall Construct hard edge around regeneration zone					
Lining Underliner Fit underliner non woven geotextile Lay liner over underliner					

Bill of Quantities contd.

Description	Quantity	Unit	Cost		
			Labour & Sub-contractors	Materials	Total
Plumbing					
Install pipework in regeneration zone					
Install pump chamber, pump filter, skimmers					
Connect water supply					
Electrical					
Electrical connections to pump chamber					
Install underwater lights					
Elements					
Deck "Boardwalk"					
Ladders					
Steps					
Jetty					
Bridge					
Waterfall					
Stream					
Planting					
Lay substrate in regeneration zone					
Plants marginal and aquatics					
Finishing					
Regrade surrounds by machine or by hand					
Seed or turf surrounds					

LEGAL

In Respect of Health and Safety

Every property owner is subject to the legal duty to maintain safety, and this also extends to private natural pools. This legal duty to maintain safety applies both during the construction phase and after completion of the natural pool. The owner of the property has the primary responsibility. During the construction phase, the person to whom the management of the site has been transferred (i.e., the planning expert or contractor) is also responsible in addition to the property owner.

There is no duty to maintain legal safety in the face of persons who access the property without being authorized. However, this does not apply to children. To reduce the risks to children, it must usually be ensured that children cannot gain access to the property, nor have an accident in the pool, e.g., by bounding the property.

Pools on private property—regardless of the type and size—represent a hazard, particularly for small children.

Every property owner must take effective and lasting measures to protect children against accidents. If he knows or should know that they use his property—whether authorized or not—for play there is a risk that they could be harmed in the process.

Safety measures must be correspondingly more effective the greater the allure exerted by the pool on children (e.g., splashing brook, stepping stones).

Absolute protection against any abstract danger does not have to be provided. Safety measures are only required that would be deemed sufficient by an intelligent and cautious person to protect other persons against harm and could be reasonably expected of him under the circumstances.

It is not automatically necessary to erect an insurmountable obstacle. A hedge or comparable barrier is sufficient in principle if children have not played on the property so far without being authorized and if the property is clearly and unambiguously set apart from the remaining terrain. If despite all warnings and instructions neighbouring children repeatedly enter the garden, special precautions will need to be taken.

Warning signs are not sufficient as a rule, as small children cannot read them.

Owners of a natural pool are recommended to take out third party liability insurance or to inform their existing insurance provider about the natural pool.

3

BUILDING

SITE PREPARATION

The Site

ACTION

Ensure the site is free of all obstacles and is ready for this first stage, including access for heavy machinery and equipment.

Consider access restraints, such as underground services and overhead cables.

Locate areas for excavated material and for the storage of machinery and equipment.

Setting Out

From the survey plan, mark on the ground the location of any underground service, such as drains, water pipes, telephone and electric cables, etc.

Using the setting out plan for the project, transfer the shape and layout of the pool to the ground using pegs or canes at all key positions. Do not confuse these with pegs indicating levels, as this will come later.

Locate the survey datum point and the other fixed reference points. Drive in pegs and mark the tops with white paint so they can be seen.

Measure from a selected fixed point of reference every important point of the pool outline. Drive in pegs and mark the tops with white paint.

Take a rope or garden hosepipe and lay out the shape very roughly until it

corresponds with the design. It can easily be adjusted at this stage if it does not look right.

Once the shape has been agreed use spray paint on the ground next to the rope or hosepipe to ensure it is recorded.

Also mark the location of the regeneration zone, the pump house/store, skimmers, filters, and deck.

Establish the desired water level from a site datum point from which it can be recalculated 100mm below existing ground level on a flat site. For a sloping site, exercise a cut and fill process and select an average level.

Edge

Before you continue the excavation, you must ensure the edge of the pool is the same height everywhere. Using one of your chosen reference points, measure from this point the height chosen for the pool edge, employing the graduated measurements mentioned. Once one point for the edge has been marked with a peg, put in further pegs at certain distances along the pool edge. A plumb line and spirit level will help you keep the pegs at the right height (but the use of a laser is better).

Once the pool's edge has been established at the right height in its

Photo: Oase

a level area at the pool edge where the water depth has been created by removing the topsoil and is 20-30cm. This strip can be 50-80cm wide, or even more if there is room for an even larger marshy area.

Now mark out another outline for the excavation of the next layer. You will probably be getting to the deepest part of the vegetation area: to 60, 80, or even 100cm. The transfer from the shallow to deep zone should be sloped gently, e.g., 1:3. The platforms don't need to be level, but can slope gently towards the centre of the pool. Keep the lower levels of soil excavated separate from the topsoil in their own area. Retain topsoil for reuse after construction.

When you have smoothed the base, mark out the outline of the intended bathing area. Include the division between this area and the water planting zone, as well as a 50cm wide working space that will be needed when constructing the dividing wall. It will need to be filled in again afterwards.

Ensure that the regeneration zone is a minimum of 2m wide.

surroundings, continue removing the next level of the pool basin. Keep a check on the accuracy of the level of the pool edge and lower areas while you are excavating until you are ready to begin laying the liner. The pool basin should fall away gently from the shoreline, just like a natural pool.

To give the plants a better hold it is a good idea to lay the slope in the vegetation area in small platforms. Leave

EXCAVATION

ACTION

Remove all topsoil from the whole of the natural swimming pool area and any other areas where it could be damaged by site works machinery and equipment.

Store topsoil in the area designated in heaps no more than 2.0 metres in height.

Set out the pool perimeter again and mark a second line of excavation.

Commence operations at the deep end (2.4m deep) and work towards the shallow end (1m deep) for ease of exit for the digger machine.

Reduce the area of excavation to 1m below datum level, removing all material to the storage area or off site.

Grade back from the inner excavation line to the ground level and outer excavation line, as shown on the working drawing on page 36.

Photo: Manzke Beton

Set out the line of separation wall by scaling off the drawing or reading measurements shown, marking the ground with spray paint.

Set out the inner dig line to define 2m or more for the deep area and mark with spray paint.

Continue excavation and form a 1:1 batter as before.

In the base of the pool excavate a 500 × 500 × 600mm deep area for the sump.

Remove all sharp stones and objects, as well as any intruding roots, boulders, etc., and compact the ground using a pounder machine.

Using a flat spade trim the sides by hand where necessary.

Allow for 50–100mm of sand to cover the base.

NOTES

Using a larger machine will aid in accurately digging within the marked outside lines. This can achieve the work of excavating an average pool (70–90 sq.m) in four to six hours compared to a smaller machine, such as a mini digger, which could take double the time.

Excavation should be undertaken when the ground is hard and firm; when it is very soft machinery can cause considerable damage to the site/garden well beyond the pool area.

Be aware that this work is unsightly and does cause considerable mess, but it is only temporary and is soon restored to normal.

Ensure that the swimming zone excavations are square. This may sound obvious, but it is very important and many mistakes are eliminated by proper 'squaring'. If it is not square it can become a 'visual nuisance'. Keep checking your measurements and ensure that all right angles are accurate.

For very small gardens with restricted access for large machinery, the use of a mini-excavator will be necessary. Unfortunately its reach (arm) is limited by its small size, so you will need to approach the proposed hole from several sides, adding to the compaction of the site. After a certain depth is reached you can no longer access the hole from the sides and if you take the machine into the hole by a ramp, the deeper the hole becomes the more difficult it is to excavate the soil. It is suited to pools less than 1.50 metres in depth.

Check the efficiency of the digger before hiring it.

If the soil is to be removed from the site or dumped some distance away a dump truck will be necessary.

Remember that excavated soil takes up more space by 25%, so a 100m^3 can easily become 125m^3 or more, depending on the soil type and conditions.

Drivers of equipment are used to excavations for buildings, roads, etc., and are not usually experienced in creating the right conditions for swimming pools, let alone a natural one. They will need to be given clear instructions.

Use tarpaulins to cover the work and protect it from heavy rain.

GROUND DRAINAGE

Under Base (French) Drain

ACTION

Excavate a 200 × 200mm trench through the floor of the pool to the drainage sump location as shown on the drawing.

Install 110mm diameter perforated land drainage pipe and backfill with 20mm diameter shingle.

If the soil is sand or other loose material line the trench with a geotextile membrane or fleece.

Connect the land drainage pipe to the pool base outlet sump.

Lay solid 160mm diameter PVC pipe from the base outlet sump to the drainage sump and connect.

NOTES

The under base drain draws groundwater away from the base and helps keep the pool work area clean and dry during construction. It is a vital part of the pool's operation, as after the pool is built it will continue to draw groundwater away from under the base. This water should be directed elsewhere in the garden.

The water in the soil can exert upward and inward pressure on the pool shell, causing flexible linings to balloon or 'hippo' upward.

There are two ways of dealing with this. The first is to build the pool above the water table. It will be essential to combine this with the modelling and grading of the ground in the surrounding areas.

If the pool is to be built below the water table, you may find it necessary to pump out water during the excavation and construction process. Dig out a small deep hole to act as a sump. As water collects it is pumped out to a place where it cannot seep back into the hole. A small submersible sump is ideal for this work.

The second way is to install permanent drainage to the ground surrounding the pool by the use of field drain pipes in trenches directed to an outlet or soakaway. Very few areas are constantly receiving such a high rainfall that a

Photo: Fairwater Ltd – Bionova

Photo: Stefan Lehnert – Bioteich

simple drainage system cannot cope with it. However, if you do have a very high water table a pump will be necessary so that water can be removed faster than it seeps back in.

If water is excessive, it may be necessary to install a land drainage system under the liner with a pipe to a manhole and pump chamber.

Perimeter (Curtain) Drain

ACTION

Lay perforated land drain in the void behind the concrete block wall around the entire pond perimeter terminating in a suitable drainage location or soakaway and cover with gravel.

Alternatively excavate a trench 150-300mm, line with geotextile, and fill with gravel.

NOTES

The perimeter drain assists in removing excessive rainwater and melting snow that otherwise will enter the pool and affect the pH.

This run-off can also carry nutrients or weed killer from other parts of the garden, which should be avoided at all costs.

Photo: Fairwater Ltd – Bionova

LINING

Underliner

ACTION

Check once again that the area is free from any debris, sharp stones, etc.

Lay sand to a depth of 50mm and compact.

Lay underliner (geotextile/fleece) across the entire excavated area.

Overlap each piece by 100mm to ensure complete coverage.

Tack or tape the strips together to prevent them from dragging apart.

Allow for 100mm to overlap the top edge so that it can be trimmed and tucked under the liner and go behind the perimeter wall.

Where the sides are steep secure the underliner to the edge of the wall position to stop it from slipping.

NOTES

The amount of material required is determined by multiplying the length of the pool by the width, plus an extra 15% for curvature and overlap.

The underliner should be unrolled from the middle of the excavated area.

Laying the underliner is relatively easy and quick to undertake, but it is nevertheless a very important part of the whole construction process. Attention to detail and taking care while working will ensure an excellent base for the installation of the liner.

In some circumstances a 100mm layer of reinforced concrete is poured over the base to ensure a very smooth and flat surface. The underliner is still used prior to the liner.

Photo: Anglo Swimming Ponds

Photo: Anglo Swimming Ponds

LINER

ACTION

Draw up a sketch of the pool area very carefully.

Give the sketch to a representative of the liner supply company so estimates can be obtained for the complete supply of the liner, including all cutting and jointing.

Working from the centre of the base, unroll and unfold the liner, ensuring all creases are gathered into one single fold and the surface is as smooth as possible.

Once the floor and lower slopes are lined, loosely lay the liner across the floor of the regeneration zone, ensuring there is sufficient material to reach the maximum water level and the trench, as well as allowing for the wall, if it is going to be exposed.

Roll the liner back onto the regeneration zone ledge, protecting it with off cuts of underliner while the wall is constructed.

If the wall is going to be covered with the liner then take it over the wall and into the regeneration area.

If the walls to the swimming zone are full height then take the liner from the base and crease it at the wall base. Standing on the liner, take it up and over the wall onto the floor of the regeneration zone, ensuring there is sufficient material to reach maximum water level and the perimeter trench.

Lay liner over the slope of the regeneration area and protect it with a second layer of underliner.

Stand underliner and liner up behind the perimeter wall and secure with concrete haunching. Trim liners to the top of the edge blocks.

NOTES

The weight of a liner that has been tailor made in one piece is considerable and requires several people to handle it.

Use a tractor to take it to the deepest point of the pool, hanging the roll on the hydraulic forks.

Several people will be required to pull the liner out while the tractor is reversed by the driver. Extreme care must be taken not to damage the liner, especially where machinery is involved.

Photo: Anglo Swimming Ponds

Where heavy liner sections are unfolded and spread out they have to be welded together. This can only be done when climatic conditions are suitable—dry and no frosts.

Specialist companies can undertake the sealing of the sections on site. This

has the advantage of the liner being cut precisely for the existing layout and eliminates all the folds. The specialists will also check it for leaks and if necessary reseal it.

If laying the liner yourself, you will undoubtedly have folds to contend with; all you can do is to reduce them in number. Try to form a large fold at one of the places where a fold is inevitable. Folds, unless done neatly, can look unsightly and even harbour debris, leaves, etc.

On arrival, inspect the liner roll thoroughly, checking for any outward appearances of damage that may have occurred in transit. Reject the liner if you have any doubts and ask the supplier to send a representative to check it. They may well accept your photographic evidence by e-mail.

Check footwear before working on the liner, ensuring there are no stones or sharp objects on shoe soles. Better still, change to a smooth-sole footwear.

Edge

The liner's edge also has the role of a capillary block. The last 10cm of the liner is vertical so that the eventual water level will have no contact with the surrounding earth. If there was contact, then in dry weather the earth would suck moisture from the pool and the water level would drop considerably—at a time when water is already being lost through evaporation. Fill in behind with topsoil and from inside the pool with a layer of gravel. If you want to be really efficient, place horizontal edging logs or concrete edging blocks on the edge. You can then pull the liner over these and finish it off at their top. When the pool is full of water and the plants are in place, cut off any edge of the liner that can be seen level with the ground.

It is essential not to have any liner showing, as it will deteriorate if exposed to ultraviolet light.

WALLS

At the project planning stage you should have decided if the pool will be built with full- or half depth walls for the separation of the two zones, along with the type of materials to be used.

The geology, soils, and ground conditions will play a part in this decision. If the type of subsoil is sandy or loose it is better to construct the wall on the base of the swimming zone and build it to the desired height. This will be a full-height wall.

FULL-DEPTH WALLS

For structural reasons, let the side walls of the swimming zone have a slight slope or batter.

To construct a full-height wall you will need to excavate a working space that has to be filled in again before the liners are laid. Fill in carefully and carefully compact the material every 250/300mm. This should be undertaken using a motorised French hammer, not by hand. If it is not compacted carefully and properly, over time the weight of the substrate and water will cause this ground to sink and stretch the liner. The liner can only give a little before ripping at the edge of the wall.

Full-height walls can be constructed from reinforced *in situ* concrete, concrete blocks, used railway sleepers and telegraph poles, gabions (wire baskets filled with gravel/rubble), or large natural stone boulders. All these are then covered with the underliner and top liner.

A natural stone boulder wall could be built inside the liner, depending on its geology.

Photo: Fairwater Ltd – Bionova

Granite, for example, could have too many sharp projections either for under or over the liner. Also, some boulders could cause the pH of the water to become more alkaline if they are taken from limestone quarries.

A boulder wall will need to be carefully built to ensure stability and safety, but keep any cement to a minimum if it has to be used.

For the builder, the easiest walls to construct are concrete block and built to a formal pattern or layout. Boulder walls are useful where the design of the swimming zone is informal.

At the other extreme, a wall can be made of compacted earth with sloping sides, provided there is sufficient space available.

ACTION

Most of these walls are covered by the liners. Consult with a structural engineer regarding reinforcing.

Solid Concrete

Make wooden shuttering to the correct size and ensure it is able to cope with vibrated concrete. Insert reinforcing mesh cut to size with bolt cutters. Allow 50mm coverage.

This work is usually done in sections.

Pour concrete either made on site in your own mixer or obtained from a concrete premix supplier.

Pound the concrete with timber log every 200mm layer to ensure compaction.

Ensure reinforcement is completely covered with a minimum of 50mm on all sides and top.

Remove shuttering and ensure there are no sharp edges protruding that could damage the liner.

Concrete Block

Excavate for footings of at least 300 × 300mm, fill with concrete, and allow for vertical reinforcing rods.

Lay hollow blocks using 1:3 mortar mix to the correct height. Check both the vertical and horizontal with laser on every course. Allow for horizontal reinforcing bars where necessary—consult an engineer.

Photo: Anglo Swimming Ponds

Fill the hollow blocks every three or four courses and pound with a timber log to ensure compaction.

Ensure there are no sharp edges that could damage the liner.

Solid Timber

Used railway sleepers, building beams, or telephone or electricity poles can be utilised to make full depth retaining walls.

Excavate for footings at least 350mm width × 300mm depth, fill with concrete, and allow for vertical reinforcing rods at 1200mm centres (approximate).

Drill holes in timber sleepers, poles, beams, etc., at above centres and place in position over the reinforcing rods. Ensure the next layer is over a joint.

Tie the back wall from the rear to a 'deadman' anchor at one metre height intervals using galvanised steel wire and staples.

Natural Stone Boulders

Excavate for footings and fill with concrete.

Place the largest boulders on the footings and build up the wall, ensuring that all joints are staggered. Ensure a minimum batter of 1:6

If you cannot achieve a stabilised wall solely with the boulders you are using, then it might be necessary to use cement mortar to make a more secure connection between them. In some circumstances, such as when the gaps are large, it will be better to use concrete.

Fill the space between the wall and the ground with hardcore and compact in layers. Allow for drainage at the base.

As this boulder wall will be covered by the liner, ensure there are no sharp projections that could cause any damage.

NOTES

A natural boulder wall could be built inside the liner, but considerable care will be required, not only in the placement of the boulders to ensure no damage, but also in their appearance. The joints will need to be very small and preferably cement-free.

Please see chapter 10 (Construction Details) for scale drawings of these walls and also *Landscape Detailing Vol 1* for specifications and technical information.

HALF-DEPTH WALLS

If the soil is heavy or stony but stable and firm, you can construct the dividing wall on the edge of the regeneration zone. This will be a half-height wall.

There is a greater choice of materials for these walls: natural stone coursed or

uncoursed, gravel sacks, railway sleepers, telegraph poles, used building beams, etc. Prefabricated units made of timber and recycled plastic are also used.

If you decide to make a wall of timber inside the liner then use seasoned larch or white pine or Douglas fir, as they will be no longer losing resin. The

Photo: Stefan Lehnert – Bioteich

of all types and phosphate is the main limiting nutrient for algal growth. Not only does concrete provide a suitable surface for algal attachment, but phosphate is released into the water that comes into contact with the concrete, enriching the water and promoting unicellular and filamentous algal growth in other parts of the system. We would always recommend that concrete ponds are lined.'

Dr. Jonathan Newman

ACTION

Exposed Walls (not covered by the liner)

These can be constructed from virtually any material that has the strength to retain the substrate and does not contaminate the water.

Natural Stone

Lay a concrete footing at the front of the regeneration zone on compacted ground or hardcore.

The underliner and liner go on top of the footing. Place another piece of underliner over the liner from the edge of the swimming zone all the way up to the perimeter wall for protection.

wood under water does not require any preservative treatment as it is not exposed to changes from wet to dry states.

NOTES

'In our experience rendered concrete tanks have to be treated with a photocatalytic paint to inhibit algae growth on tank walls. The coatings only work in the light, so any shaded areas would always be covered in algae, regardless of the coating. Concrete is a good substrate for algal growth because it is usually rough and contains phosphate. The rough surface promotes adherence of algae

Photo: Fairwater Ltd – Bionova

Lay the stone—coursed or uncoursed, or even dressed—as shown in the construction detail drawings.

Geotextile Bags

Fill the bags with smooth gravels—mixed size—and secure. Where possible, use recycled rubble for filling geotextile bags, but ensure protection of the liner by using two sheets of underliner.

Lay the bags on compacted ground or on a concrete footing lengthways, with the occasional one at right angles.

Screw boards or planks to the frame. Dowel capping board to the top of the units.

Non-Exposed Walls (covered by the liner)

Rounded/Square Timber Logs/Beams

Lay a concrete footing 300mm depth × 400mm width, inserting vertical steel rods every 1200mm.

Drill holes in logs and lay over vertical steel rods.

Ensure that subsequent layers overlap all joints.

Lay underliner and liner over the timber wall.

Recycled Plastic Units

At the present time these are made solely by Biotop, although they may consider selling these or for them to be made under licence in the future. A different design may well be forthcoming that does not infringe any patent rights.

Ensure the bags overlap the joints on each layer and that there is a slight batter, or that the bags are set back at the start of the next row.

Timber Frame Units

Make up frames as shown on the construction detail drawing.

Lay a concrete footing 300mm depth by 400mm width over the liner, using pieces of underliner to provide protection. Also cover the footing with underliner and liner where it is exposed to the water.

Secure timber frame supports to the concrete footing with stainless steel screw bolts. Bolt units together.

PERIMETER WALL

ACTION

This wall is built around the edge of the pool—particularly the regeneration zone—and is also formed to create a capilliary barrier, preventing water from accidentally seeping in and out of the pool. Ensure that it is built 100mm higher than water level.

Depending on the shape and layout of the pool, the walls can also be built of concrete linear units, timber strips and pegs, timber planks, or flexible metal strips and steel pegs. Alternatively, the ground can be shaped to the correct profile to create a small mound.

Concrete Block Wall

Before pulling underliner and liner out from behind the separation wall, excavate a 300 × 300mm level edge at the top of the regeneration zone slope.

Pour a concrete footing onto the ledge.

Lay underliner and liner over the slope of the regeneration zone and protect with a second layer of underliner.

Lay a single course of concrete blocks 225 × 100 × 450mm, ensuring they are 100mm above maximum datum water level.

Stand liners up behind blocks and secure with concrete haunching. Trim liners to the top of the wall.

Photo: R. Willer

Photo: Fairwater Ltd – Bionova

POOL CONVERSIONS

Photo: GartenArt Ltd

Many people are unaware that the conversion of a traditional pool can easily be undertaken, provided there is sufficient space around it for aquatic plants. A large part of the construction—namely the excavation and the removal of all the surplus soil and debris—has already been done. The pool has probably been built with either concrete or concrete blocks and rendered. It will probably have coping and paving slabs surrounding it and these can be removed completely to a safe place. Some could be re-used.

If it has been decided to keep the size of the existing pool for swimming then the regeneration zone must be made about the same area. If not, then the pool area could be sub divided by building new walls.

The surrounding ground will need to be excavated and the correct profile used for the regeneration zone and for filling with special substrate.

To ensure that no water collects between the liners and concrete floor of the pool a drainage system will need to be installed, with provision for an outlet pipe to a soakaway. There is an outlet drain in the base of most conventional pools and this can also be used for emptying and cleaning.

This is followed by the pipework for inlet and outlet, with connections to the skimmer and the pump.

A timber or stone coping should be fixed on top of the walls of the pool to provide a neat trim that will also help hold the liner in place. The substrate is placed in position, followed by the planting of the aquatic plants and finally, the whole area is filled with water.

At least the conversion process does not have the same upheaval going on in the garden as for a new pool.

Photo: Woodhouse Natural Pools Ltd

SUBSTRATE

For protection in the regeneration zone, place a second layer of underliner over the liner.

Lay clean washed marine shingle 10–30mm marine shingle to a depth of 100mm across the base of the entire zone.

Lay 100mm diameter perforated pipes on top of the shingle. They should be coiled or branched to cover as much of the base area as possible. Attach pipes to the liner using welded straps

Stand the balancing tank or distribution chamber in a central position on the substrate.

Terminate one end of each pipe in the balancing tank. Seal the open end of each pipe away from the balancing tank with a suitable end stop, ensuring water is forced out along its length.

Cover pipes with more shingle to 400mm below the separation wall, grading up to within 100mm of the perimeter edge block.

Once planting has been done, dress with a layer of 20mm shingle to neaten.

NOTES

Ensure material is kept free from dust and other contaminants if stored on site in heaps. Alternatively, order in large bags and hoist into position.

The substrate should not be coarse or too fine. Gravel is readily available in various sizes. Sometimes lava, pumice, vermiculite, and clay are added. Seek expert advice before ordering.

Remember, the substrate is subject to water flow from above or below, or parallel to the pool floor of the regeneration zone. If the substrate mix is too fine it can slow down the flow far too much.

The main aim is to get water to flow slowly enough through the substrate to provide nutrients for the plants but not so slowly that it may cause algae to form.

4

PLUMBING

PUMPS

Pumps should be robust, protected from water spray, quiet, easy to use and maintain, energy efficient, and provide suction.

A transparent inspection lid in the suction compartment—in which there is also a fine filter—is an advantage. The pump should be of good quality, with important metal parts of stainless steel, plastic wheels, and sliding ring joints of carbon and ceramic.

Strong pumps (230 V/380 V) should be installed according to manufacturer instructions and legal requirements. To obtain maximum efficiency they should be close to the area of operation, but at least 3m from the pool.

The water volume that the pump has to cope with daily or hourly has to be calculated for the size of the pool and items of equipment.

It is a good idea to have the pump sited below the water level, so that air is not sucked in. A stopcock should be installed on the suction side, so the pump can be dismantled, overhauled, or removed for the winter. On the pressure side it also needs a valve, so there is no back flow of water and the efficiency of the pump can be regulated.

The pump has a filter basket on the inlet to collect any debris. Since the pump is set to run automatically, it is vital to ensure the control panel is switched off before checking the filter basket. Close the inlet and outlet valves and unscrew the filter cap. Care should be taken when replacing to ensure the O-ring locates and seals correctly.

The pump is protected by a float switch positioned in the filter chamber. Should the filter become blocked, the switch will prevent the pump running when no water is available.

Types of Pumps

SUBMERSIBLE UNDERWATER PUMPS are put into the water. After the pump has been inserted they suck up the water and force it up to the source. They are low maintenance, quiet, and sturdy. They can be left in the water, but should be removed from the water in winter if long term freezing occurs in your area.

Always pull the pump itself out—never pull on the cable. Place pumps on a stand so they do not suck up any sludge. Underwater pumps are mainly used for streams and waterfalls.

This type of pump can be used in the swimming or regeneration zone, provided it does not exceed 24 volts.

SURFACE PUMPS – A standard type of swimming pool circulation pump is recommended. This should be a reputable make with quality components, but does not have to be expensive. It is often called a 'surface pump' since it is designed to be out of the water with a suction pipe inlet and discharge pipe outlet. The pump assembly is normally a pump unit with an integral filter basket on the inlet to remove larger solids and an impeller to drive to the outlet.

It is coupled to an electric motor that is insulated from the pump, making it electrically safe. Try to select a self-priming pump that will cope with the stop/start duty required for a natural pool.

For most domestic pools a single-phase 230-volt pump is sufficient. On larger installations it may be more efficient to have a three-phase pump that consumes less electricity, but this will depend on the supply available to the property (larger houses may have a three-phase supply). Another important factor to check is that the pump is 'continuously rated', meaning it can run constantly if required. This may be necessary when commissioning the pool in the summer, when constant circulation is needed to combat the initial growth of algae when a pool is filled from the mains water supply.

A chemical pool requires the pump to run for considerable periods to ensure the water receives sufficient chlorine to prevent algae growing. This is very different from a natural pool, where the water is being filtered by plants, gravel, and naturally occurring bacteria. In a natural pool circulation is kept to a minimum, allowing the water to gently circulate and let natural processes take place at their own speed.

Calculation Example:

A pool has a swimming zone of

$10m \times 5m \times 2m$ deep $= 100m^3$.

The regeneration zone is the same area, but has an average depth of

$0.3m = 15m^3$.

The total volume of the pool (including pipework, filters, etc.) is about $120m^3$ of water.

A pump delivering $13.5m^3$ per hour circulating the water for 4 hours per day is sufficient. This equates to a daily circulation rate of $54m^3$ per day. Therefore, the total water body will be turned over in just over 2 days; quite different to the turnover rate of a chemically dosed pool.

Assuming the pump has a 230-volt single-phase motor it will have a running current of about 3.5 amps. Simplifying the calculation to its most basic:

Power watts = volts $\times$ amps

The pump will use

230 (volts) $\times$ 3.5 (amps) = 805 watts =

0.8 kilowatts.

If the pump runs for 4 hours per day the consumption will be:

0.8 (kw) $\times$ 4 (hrs) = 3.2 kilowatt hours. Check your electric bill to see how much this will cost. An average electric fire runs at about 3kw per hour!

Pipe Sizes

A typical pool pump has pipe connections of 38mm or 50mm. As a 'rule of thumb', the outlet pipe size should not exceed the inlet pipe, although the inlet can be larger than the outlet. This is because it is more difficult to suck up water than it is to pump it under pressure.

For most installations, it will be sufficient to use a suction pipe of 50mm (reduce to 38mm at the pump if necessary). The delivery or outlet pipe can be 50mm as well, since this delivers the water at a steady, less pressurised rate. If the outlet pipework is reduced in size the water will be delivered under more pressure, rather like putting your thumb over the end of a hosepipe. This is not desirable when discharging into the regeneration zone since it may disturb the gravel layers.

Location

The pump is housed in a pump chamber outside the pool.

Frequency of Use

The pool circulation system is set up for average use of a few hours per day. The entire water contents of the pool will pass through the filters every two to three days. If heavy usage is anticipated it may be necessary to increase pump running time to ensure good water quality. This is easily achieved by amending the time clock programme.

Maintaining the balance is not a precise science and needs to be judged by the quality of the water. If it deteriorates, then increase the circulation time. Conversely, a retired couple may only need to run the pump twice a week if there is little pool use. Don't be afraid to adjust settings to obtain the best results. After all, it is a matter of personal preference.

Pump Selection

When selecting a pump, it is advisable to seek help from a specialist supplier. You will need to be able to answer the following questions, where relevant:

Is the pump required to operate a watercourse, fountain, or filter, or a combination of the three?

What is the volume of the reservoir pool? The flow rate per hour should not exceed the pool's volume.

For features where water runs downhill, what is the height of the header pool above the reservoir pool (know as the 'head')?

What is the width of any stream and spillway?

What type of fountain spray is required?

How high do you require the spray to be?

Flow Rate – Rough Guide

If you can achieve the desired flow of water over a fall or down a stream using a hose, then keeping the same flow rate, time how long it takes the hose to fill a container of known capacity. You can use this to estimate the flow rate required of the pump. For example, if it fills a 100 litre container in 10 minutes, then a pumping rate of 10 litres per minute will be required.

If you want to make a stream flow and operate in a larger pool you will need a stronger pump (10,000, 20,000, or 30,000 litres per hour capacity). The water is sucked along pipes from the deeper part to the outside area of the pool, where it will flow back into the pool in the form of a stream or waterfall.

Photo: Carsten Schmidt

PUMP CHAMBER

There are ready-made chambers in which the pumps are already installed and fitted with pipes and ball taps. They are placed at a suitable location so that no water can enter from above.

Concrete rings (e.g., 100cm inside diameter and 60cm high) can also be suitable for pump chambers. They must be located where water cannot penetrate from above or below. Usually this chamber is provided with a drainage pipe so that water can flow away if necessary. It is best to use an excavator or lorry with a claw to position the 100-kilo ring after putting down leveled gravel or bricks for the ring to stand on.

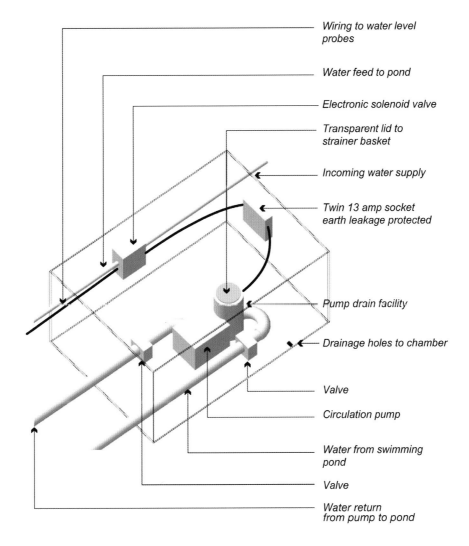

- Wiring to water level probes
- Water feed to pond
- Electronic solenoid valve
- Transparent lid to strainer basket
- Incoming water supply
- Twin 13 amp socket earth leakage protected
- Pump drain facility
- Drainage holes to chamber
- Valve
- Circulation pump
- Water from swimming pond
- Valve
- Water return from pump to pond

Pump Chamber Isometric   Scale:NTS

A rippled aluminium lid makes a good cover. It can be hidden by a cover of pebbles, bark mulch, or something similar. Pipes leading to and from the shaft can be built in from below, or holes can be drilled into the concrete and foam placed around the pipes when fitted.

Insulate the chamber, as pumps can make a noise that can be irritating, even when located some distance from the pool.

ACTION

Construct the chamber 1000 × 1000 × 500 mm deep and locate close to or adjacent to the filter chamber.

Ensure the bottom drain is connected to a suitable drainage pipe, as the chamber must remain dry.

Connect the pump inlet marked 'suction' or 'flow' to the suction hose from the filter chamber.

Connect a second 50mm pipe to the 'outlet' or 'return' of the pump and lay this 450mm below ground to the distribution/balancing tank in the regeneration zone.

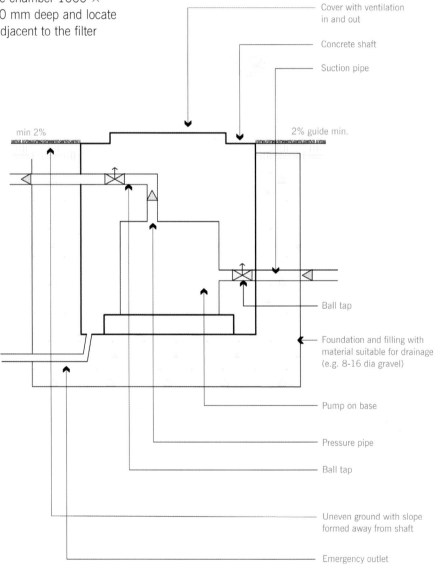

Cover with ventilation in and out

Concrete shaft

Suction pipe

min 2%

2% guide min.

Ball tap

Foundation and filling with material suitable for drainage (e.g. 8-16 dia gravel)

Pump on base

Pressure pipe

Ball tap

Uneven ground with slope formed away from shaft

Emergency outlet

Pump House Concrete

Scale: NTS

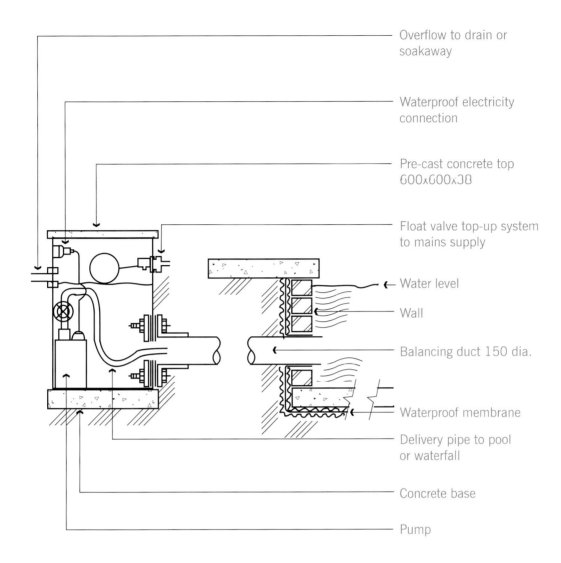

Overflow to drain or soakaway

Waterproof electricity connection

Pre-cast concrete top 600x600x38

Float valve top-up system to mains supply

← Water level

Wall

Balancing duct 150 dia.

Waterproof membrane

Delivery pipe to pool or waterfall

Concrete base

Pump

Pump Chamber – External

Scale 1:20

FILTER CHAMBER

It is usual but not essential to place the filter chamber beneath an access trap in a decked area. Alternatively, it could be located away from the pool beneath steel or timber doors.

It consists of a stainless steel perforated cylinder covered with a geotextile filter cloth. Around the outside of the filter are four fleece cartridges containing a special medium to assist with phosphate removal and a bacterial growth promoter.

Water from the pool skimmer enters in the filter centre and flows to the outside

via gravity. A healthy filter will have inner and outer water levels more or less the same, although there may be a slight difference in levels when the pump is running. As the filter becomes clogged the water level inside the cylinder will be much higher than the outside, since the passage through the filter cloth is now restricted. The cloth should be removed and cleaned or replaced.

To clean the cloth, squeeze and rinse in fresh water, changing the water as necessary. It will be very cloudy at first and should become less so at each water

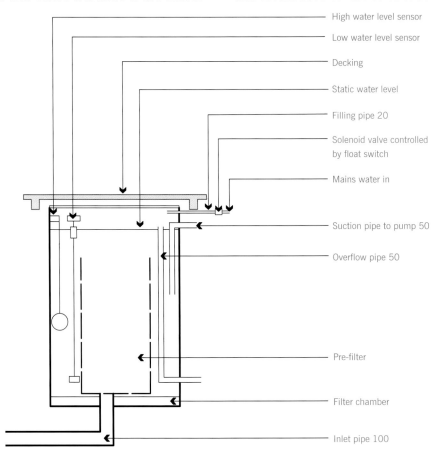

High water level sensor

Low water level sensor

Decking

Static water level

Filling pipe 20

Solenoid valve controlled by float switch

Mains water in

Suction pipe to pump 50

Overflow pipe 50

Pre-filter

Filter chamber

Inlet pipe 100

Plumbing – Filter Chamber   Scale: NTS

change. Do not expect the water to run completely clear. As long as the bulk of the debris has been removed this should be sufficient.

The chamber is 1.5m diameter and fully opening access is required for maintenance and removal of the pre-filter.

ACTION

Excavate a 2.0 × 2.0m hole for the filter chamber, ensuring the rim is level with the top of the perimeter wall.

Connect 100mm pipework and backfill with suitable clean graded site material.

Compact well with a mechanical compactor, ensuring that no sharp stones, etc., are allowed to pierce the structure.

Connect a 50mm suction hose or rigid pipe to the pump inlet connection and continue to the pump chamber.

Connect a suitable armoured cable to the gland provided for the automatic water level sensor. This should be on

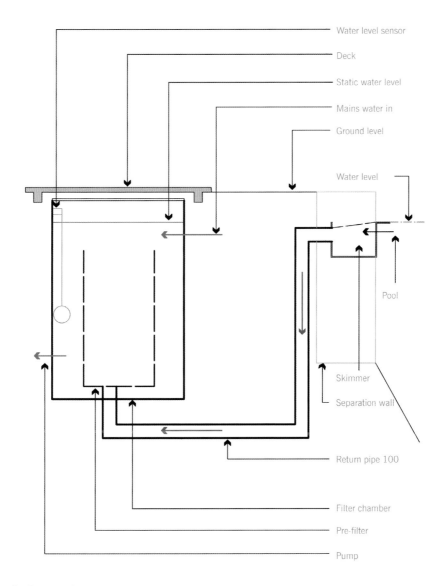

Water level sensor

Deck

Static water level

Mains water in

Ground level

Water level

Pool

Skimmer

Separation wall

Return pipe 100

Filter chamber

Pre-filter

Pump

Skimmer and Filter Schematic

Scale: NTS

the outside of the pre-filter. The reason for this is that any debris coming in via the skimmer will begin to clog the inside surface of the pre-filter. This reduces the flow; although the inside of the filter is full of water, it cannot pass to the outside because of the partial blockage so the level drops on the outside (because the pump is removing water).

The low-level float switch should be set to ensure that the suction line to the pump always has water. If the level gets too low it will turn the pump off to prevent it sucking in air.

Connect a 20mm mains water pipe to the water inlet.

Place the pre-filter over the rising inlet in the floor of the filter chamber. Install substrate cartridges into the sockets provided.

Alternatives

Another method is to use a circular container 1.50m deep; the width depends on the size of the pool. This is filled with stone chippings of several different sizes, with the largest at the bottom. The top is covered with a piece of geotextile material and then with sharp sand or very small gravel. The water is drawn through the container by the action of the pump and is then returned slowly to the regeneration zone.

In place of the stone chippings 'Zeolith' could be used. This stone is very porous and has an enlarged surface area. It is then inhabited by numerous bacteria that clean the water brought from the surface skimmer by breaking down phosphate and nitrate compounds. The pump returns the water to the pool. The water should not be pushed through the filters at too fast a speed, as it would remove plankton from the pool, causing the water to become cloudy and algae to appear.

SKIMMERS

Floating Skimmers

These have a base that is set in the pool—in it is a filter basket and if required a (foam) fine filter. On top of the base is the floating cover, which draws water from the surface and adapts to the water level. These do not affect the zooplankton that is at deeper levels, as they only skim a few millimetres at the surface. They can easily be fitted under a landing stage with an access cover. Stepping stones make them accessible, or two hooks on a pole make a home-made means of removing the sieve and the cover. Weight them down with stones when filling the pool to stop them from floating to the surface.

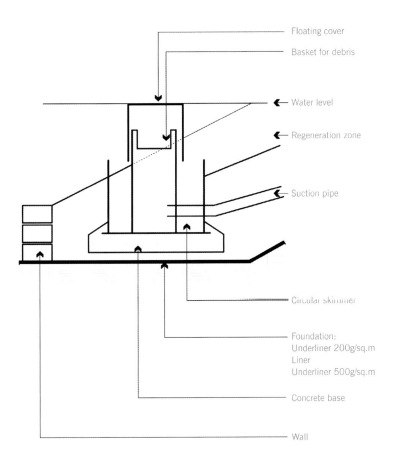

Floating cover
Basket for debris
Water level
Regeneration zone
Suction pipe
Circular skimmer
Foundation:
Underliner 200g/sq.m
Liner
Underliner 500g/sq.m
Concrete base
Wall

Note: Floating skimmers
are placed at a depth
of 500-700

Floating Skimmer   Scale: NTS

These skimmers can also be easily added afterwards if experience shows that more are needed.

There are some available with bases that can be filled with concrete.

The filters should be emptied and cleaned every one to two days, switching the pump off first. Remember that fine filters can be used to remove pollen and seeds.

Built-in Skimmers

These are placed near the bank and have a mobile lid that can tolerate a certain alteration in water levels. They are easy to maintain, but are not so efficient if plants have taken root nearby.

ACTION

Depending on the type of skimmer selected, set the lip at the desired water level, 100mm lower than the perimeter wall.

Make sure the skimmer is set level from side to side, but note that the back of the skimmer is lower than the front. This ensures that the water flows at speed across the grill.

Trim the liner to fit the flange plate on the back of the skimmer and cut holes just large enough to pass the studs through. Make sure the liner is flat against the flange back plate, without any creases.

Dress a small quantity of proprietary silicon sealant around each stud and then locate the clamping plate. Tighten the nuts—a turn past hand tight only.

Ensure the liner has not been snagged or cut and secure the entire unit with concrete haunching to the rear.

Connect 100mm PVC pipe to the socket on the back of the skimmer and turn it immediately down to level with the filter inlet as detailed. It is essential that this pipe drops vertically to guard against air locks.

Continue 100mm pipework to connection on the base of the filter chamber. All connections must be solvent-welded and not rubber push-fit.

If preferred, the skimmer may be set into the perimeter wall at the rear of the regeneration zone.

It is critical to size the pipe run from the skimmer to the pump chamber correctly, as this makes sure the flow is sufficient to keep the pump fed with water.

Animal-friendly Skimmer

Set the skimmer so that the water level is 30mm below the upper edge of the entrance. There is approximately 100mm leeway.

Animal-friendly skimmer

Access stone to skimmer

Skimmer in place, with easy access

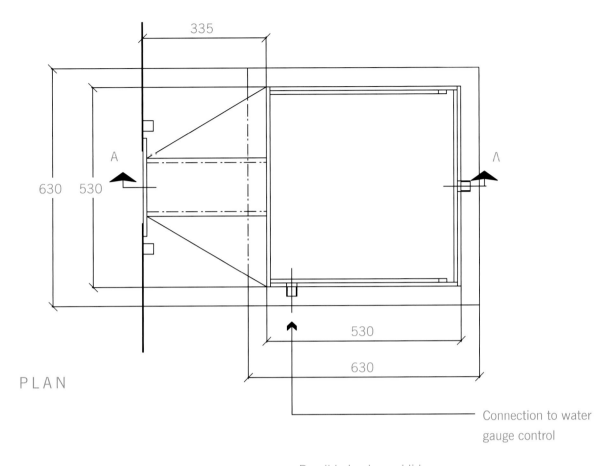

335

630 530

A

Λ

530

630

PLAN

Connection to water
gauge control

Possible larchwood lid

Possible wood covering

screen element

Water level

Skimmer
flap

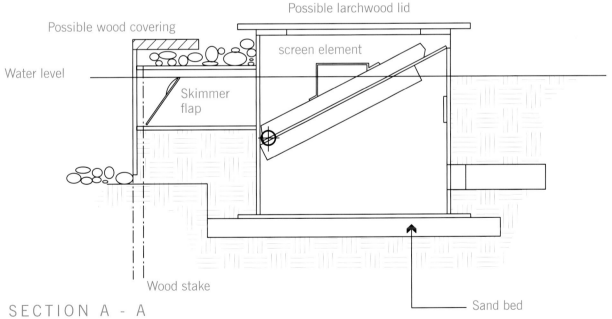

Wood stake

SECTION A - A

Sand bed

Animal-friendly Skimmer

Scale: 1:20

BALANCING TANK

A small circular chamber 450mm in diameter is situated in the regeneration zone. Water from the circulation pump is delivered here and distributed through the zone for final filtration before re-entering the main pool. No maintenance should be necessary, but the lid can be lifted to check that the pump is operating correctly. Water will be seen entering the chamber when the pump is running.

ACTION

Allow for the location of the tank in the regeneration zone in a convenient position for connection of the perforated pipes.

Make a note of the position in case access is required for future inspection, bearing in mind it will be covered with gravel when the pool is finished.

WATER LEVEL CONTROL

If an automatic water gauge control is installed then there is no need for any topping up by hand.

The efficiency should be checked from time to time to ensure it is operating successfully.

A mains water top-up valve and overflow pipe are in the main filter chamber. In some systems these are an integral unit. The valve and overflow heights are set on commissioning and should not be altered.

The addition of small amounts of mains water will not affect the quality of the natural water in the pool, since chlorine dissipates very quickly once exposed to air. It is suggested that top-up water is passed through a reed bed to purify it. Any filling or top-up water must have a total phosphorus level of <0.030mg/l on entering the pool.

ACTION

Locate in a suitable position and connect to the skimmer, ensuring that the required water level is 30mm below the upper edge of the entrance to the skimmer.

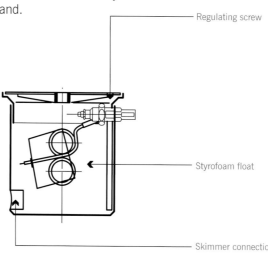

Regulating screw

Styrofoam float

Skimmer connection

Water Gauge Control

Scale: NTS

OUTLET DRAIN
(SWIMMING ZONE)

There is a depression in the bottom of the deepest part of the pool to collect soil and other sinking debris. The pipe connected to this depression has a valve that should be opened every few weeks (or as necessary) to flush away the accumulated debris and prevent it being stirred up by swimmers. It is only necessary to open the valve for a very brief time.

Take care not to stand in front of the valve unless a safety gate is installed, since the flow is very strong.

The valve can also be used to drain the pool completely. Ensure that the mains water top-up valve is switched off or you will be refilling as you empty.

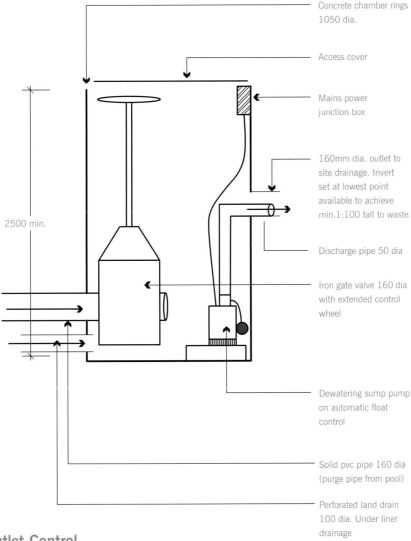

Concrete chamber rings 1050 dia.

Access cover

Mains power junction box

160mm dia. outlet to site drainage. Invert set at lowest point available to achieve min.1:100 fall to waste

Discharge pipe 50 dia

Iron gate valve 160 dia with extended control wheel

2500 min.

Dewatering sump pump on automatic float control

Solid pvc pipe 160 dia (purge pipe from pool)

Perforated land drain 100 dia. Under liner drainage

Return and Outlet Control

Scale: NTS

OVERFLOW GULLEYS

The overflow gulley works the same way that a skimmer does—drawing debris off the surface of the pool. The difference is that the gulley is fixed, so it needs careful positioning, with its surface just below water level so that leaves can flow over it.

It is usual to create a small area behind the skimmer to collect the debris for removal by hand every so often. This helps prevent the slotted cover from becoming completely blocked.

The overflow gulley is connected to the filter chamber by a 100mm pipe in the same way as a skimmer. This is shown in the next section (Pipework and Accessories).

Photo: Fairwater Ltd – Bionova

Photo: Jörg Baumhauer

PIPEWORK & ACCESSORIES

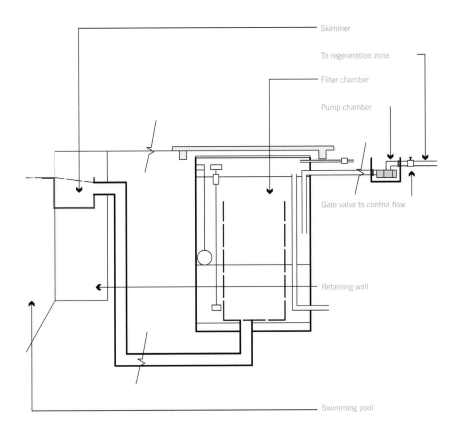

Skimmer

To regeneration zone

Filter chamber

Pump chamber

Gate valve to control flow

Retaining wall

Swimming pool

Pipework

The easiest pipe to use is a flexible one, with the ribbed version being even more flexible, although it is much more expensive.

Always select the largest practical diameter pipe with the fewest number of fittings on any run, as this will allow the pump to operate at highest efficiency.

Even so, for every 3m pipe length it will lose between 270 and 450 litres per hour in power.

Accessories

These should be from the same manufacturer as the pump, as systems can rarely be interchanged. The dimensions of the pipes should be too large rather than too small, so that the speed of flow is not too high, as this can harm the biological processes.

The inside diameter of pipes for 230V pumps with a capacity of 3,000–8,000 litres per hour should be 30–50mm; those with a capacity of 8,000–15,000 litres per hour should be 63mm, and higher capacities require stronger pipes.

Items such as PVC adhesive joints, ball taps, couplers, T-joints, etc., have stood the test of time and can be attached with spiral adhesive pipes. Note that certain items need to be frost-resistant and others need to be deep enough to be safe from frost.

WATER FLOW

The circulation pump draws water from the filter chamber, sending it to the distribution chamber in the regeneration zone via the perforated pipes. The water rises through the gravel layers and flows into the swimming zone, increasing the level. It then flows over the skimmer and returns to the filter chamber.

The flow should be such that a gentle drift is created across the pool towards the skimmer, pulling any floating debris with it. The larger particles settle on or around the skimmer for easy removal. Finer particles are filtered out by the pre-filter, while even finer ones are deposited when the water circulates back to the gravel layers of the regeneration zone. The organic particles are broken down by naturally occurring bacteria in the gravel strata. Once the nutrients and other elements are released they are taken up by the higher plants as food, thereby ensuring the water returning to the swimming zone is clean and healthy.

With use, the water in the swimming zone will become contaminated with debris, fats (as in sun screen, etc.), and other pollutants. Dirty water is heavier than clean water and sinks to the bottom. If a purge (outlet) valve system is fitted, it is useful to open the valve regularly to remove the heavy contaminated water, leaving the main body of water undisturbed.

COMMISSIONING

On commissioning, it is important to set the correct pump flow rate to ensure the system is balanced. Water is pumped to the pool, but returns through the skimmer by natural gravitational flow. This is why the return pipe is much larger than the delivery pipe, allowing for friction loss. If the pump flow is set too high it will move water faster than it can return, causing 'draw down', which is apparent by the level in the filter dropping. This makes it difficult to set the mains water top up and overflow accurately since the level can fluctuate.

When commissioning, switch the pump on and allow time for the water in the filter to reach a steady level. If this level is lower than when the pump is switched off close the delivery side valve slightly. The water level in the filter should rise. Continue making adjustments until the water is at its normal height in the filter. This is the point where flow and return are equal. Close the delivery valve a little more to compensate for any blockage occurring on the skimmer and the correct flow rate is now set. The mains water top up and overflow can be set to this water level, which should hold steady without fluctuation.

Photo: Anglo Swimming Ponds

5

ELECTRICAL

ELECTRICAL SYSTEM

General

Great care should be taken when rotation pumps or other electrical items are running, such as pumps for fountain stones and water fountains, mill stones, pool lights, or filters. The wiring should be safe and insulated. Defective circuits can be dangerous, so all equipment should be subjected to safety tests.

To conform to current regulations all 'in-pool' electrical equipment should be no more than 24 volts.

Surface (suction) pumps have an insulated coupling between the pump unit and motor, therefore higher voltages can be used.

Safety

It is essential to have a special safety fuse or breaker. The outdoor electrical supply must also be protected from blowing the whole domestic supply with a 30amp RCD trip switch that will shut things down instantly if there is any trace of power 'leaking to earth'. This would occur as soon as any dampness found its way into a connection or electrical unit, or if any current found a way out into the environment.

Only a qualified person is allowed to lay electrical circuits and connect them in order to issue a certificate 'Part P' of the regulations (UK). See 'BS 7671: 2000 Requirements for Electrical Installations Section 602 Swimming Pools'.

Materials

Only use switches, sockets, or cable connectors that are safely approved for outdoor use. All high voltage cabling must be armoured or protected by a conduit and should be attached with waterproof connectors above water level wherever possible. Switch off all equipment before handling.

Records

When laying out the cables and water systems, take photographs to keep for reference when problems arise. Then fill in, keeping a few points of reference that will always be recognisable. Slabs, bricks, or pipes will protect the underground vulnerable circuits from unintentional damage with a spade.

Controls

The control panel is designed to operate automatically. A time clock runs the circulation pump for the recommended period each day. In the event of a power outage, the time clock retains its memory and will resume normal operation when power is restored. The main switch should be turned off during winter if the pool is not in use.

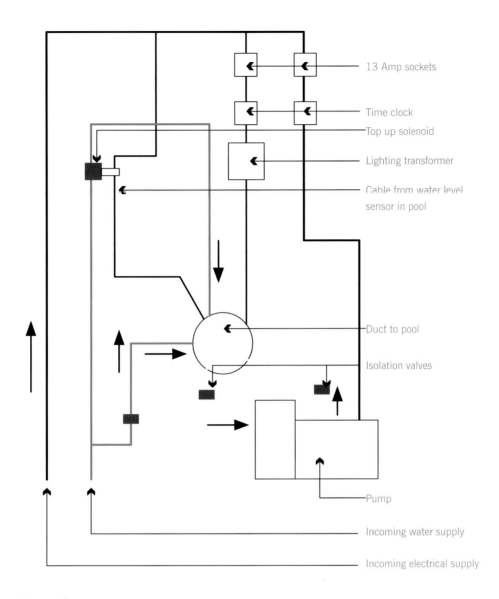

13 Amp sockets

Time clock

Top up solenoid

Lighting transformer

Cable from water level
sensor in pool

Duct to pool

Isolation valves

Pump

Incoming water supply

Incoming electrical supply

Control room schematic

Supply

To supply electricity, you can have either a single armoured cable or run an ordinary mains cable through an electrical conduit. It is important to work out the costs in advance for each one.

Armoured Cable

The size of the armoured cable you select should be capable of supplying 13 amps worth of power at 240 volts. It should be laid at a depth of 500mm set in a 150mm deep bed of clean chippings with a plastic tape warning strip lying on top. Check these regulations with an electrician, as they could change at any time.

Four-core is a popular choice for those who want to run a pump for a waterfall and fountain and a separate one for a biological filter system and still have a spare for pool lights. Where the armoured cable joins up with a cable to the unit for which you want power you will need a junction box with the correct waterproof fittings to 'translate' the armoured cable to the ordinary weatherproof cable of the unit. It is important to budget for this.

Conduit

The alternative method is to lay a conduit down to carry ordinary weatherproof domestic cable. There is a special flexible electrician's conduit, but for long runs, outdoor alkathene or plastic water pipe will do; a 25mm-bore plastic water pipe can take several cables.

You will have to consider where you want the switches. Having them near the pool makes it simpler, because there is less cable to run outside. As with the armoured cable, one cable can run them all.

If you want to run several cables through the conduit, always ensure there is a draw cord in place, because it is virtually impossible to thread more cables through when there is already some cable there.

Each time you pull through another cable ensure there is another piece of wire attached to it, because this will be a 'draw cord' you use to pull up the next cable.

Safety Requirements

It is essential to have all cabling, connections, and fittings for mains voltage pumps installed by a qualified electrician. The system must be protected by a residual current device (RCD or circuit breaker), which will cut off some of the supply instantly in the event of a short-circuit or damage.

Try to take an electrical supply from a point that is not protected by an RCD that also protects the house. This will prevent 'nuisance tripping' indoors if there is an outside fault.

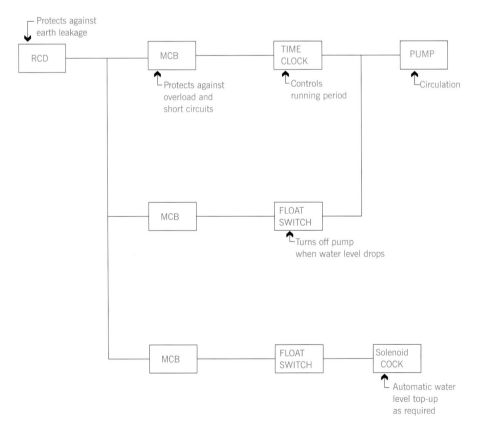

Electrical Circuit schematic

LIGHTING

Water, if lit after dark, can be quite magical.

Plant and objects that are illuminated above and around a pool will be reflected with startling clarity in the dark water.

Lighting can enhance many aspects of the natural swimming pool and different effects can be achieved either above or below the surface.

The light source—along with related cables and equipment—should never be visible.

Lamps should be well hidden behind plants, boulders, or special enclosures.

Lights should play upon the plant or object to be illuminated.

Do not let lights shine directly on to the water, as this creates an unsubtle effect.

Place lights around the sides of the pool and direct the light to the middle for the best effect.

Underwater lights can become dimmed very quickly due to coatings of algae, etc., and require periodic cleaning.

Locate controls at a convenient place, such as in the house or an easily accessible outbuilding.

Use low voltage submersible lights with a transformer in the pump house, provided it is close by. Do not exceed runs of 30m.

Select the appropriate rating for the transformer depending on the number and type of lights selected.

Select underwater light fittings that do not encourage insects in large numbers or increased weed growth. Halogen lamps are preferable to vapour.

Fibre-optic technology is suitable for underwater lighting and the light source can be located at a safe distance and be taken to wherever it is required. It is ideal for underwater use as the light is cool, meaning there is less build up of algae and scale.

Use separate circuits for waterfalls and fountains.

Protect all outside cables with a safety trip or circuit breaker.

Before final selection, conduct one or two experiments to obtain the desired effect of light on or under the water.

For an excellent text on pool lighting please refer to *Pool Scaping* by Catriona Tudor Erler (see references).

Photo: Oase, Living Water

6

STRUCTURES

STREAMS

Photo: Stefan Lehnert – Bioteich

Lay the underliner (geotextile) over the area, cutting extra pieces for placing underneath rock/boulder locations.

Lay the rubber liner beginning at the lowest section of the stream bed, overlapping by 150mm on the downhill side.

Carefully construct any waterfalls after positioning the liner, ensuring all sections are securely joined at these junctions in the stream.

Place concrete pads for the support of rocks and boulders over a piece of underlay on the liner.

Put rocks, boulders, and gravels in position, ensuring enclosures for aquatic plants.

An artificial stream will use a pump (surface or submersible) to recirculate the water; to do this, it will require a large reservoir at the bottom end. This should

Photo: Stefan Lehnert – Bioteich

Excavate the ground according to the design, ensuring the shape and depth are achieved with sensitivity.

Make allowances for boulders and rocks, both on the sides of the stream and where there are to be any changes of level.

Compact the ground; any hardcore used for filling must be covered with sand to ensure no sharp projections.

Photo: Stefan Lehnert – Bioteich

be in the form of a pond and to prevent a significant drop in level when the pump is switched on, the surface areas should be as great as the entire surface of the stream. For example, a stream 70m long by an average of 700mm wide would require a pond approximately 49m^2 or 7 × 7m (approx 400ft^2). Allowance should also be made for loss of water by evaporation, capillary action, or leakage. In certain circumstances, e.g., where the bottom pond cannot be as large as described, then the water may have to be topped up. Once the pump is switched off the stream will continue to flow down until it has reached its static level; consequently, the bottom pond could overflow unless allowance has been made for the water in the design.

A flowing stream warms the water faster, but also causes higher temperatures, which has advantages and disadvantages, so consider how long it should be in use. Now and then for a few hours is enough, and that will benefit the fauna in the pool.

Header Pools

If you are having a stream or a rill (a formal stream or mini-canal) it is necessary to have a 'header pool' for a small reservoir of water for receiving water via the delivery pipe. This will give a much better effect than if the pipe simply discharges into the start of the channel.

ACTION

The end of the delivery pipe should be above the water level of the header pool.

If the pipe discharges under water use a non-return valve to prevent siphon action.

Conceal the header pool as appropriate.

Ensure any intermediate pools are deep enough to return the water when the pump is turned off.

Design streams to empty when the pump is switched off. Algae is prone to build up in shallow pools and can then be flushed into the main pool.

103

WATERFALLS

A waterfall in a garden setting should not be too high, as it is difficult to make it look natural, depending on the landform of the site. It will be necessary to circulate a very large volume of water. There are as many types of waterfalls as there are ways of arranging rocks. The height of the fall and the type of rocks used below it will affect the sound. If it is very high it could be too noisy, cause too much splashing, and lose water too quickly.

A constant facility for topping up the water supply may be necessary.

The building of a waterfall without mortar being applied to the rocks—except where it is necessary—will ensure the effect looks as natural as possible.

By varying the shapes of rocks or boulders and the way spillways are formed, it is possible to achieve a series of waterfalls of great variety and interest at all times. The artistic flair of the designer will be paramount.

Grouting of all the waterfall rocks should be undertaken when they are in their final position, using a waterproof mix of sand and cement or self-expanding polyurethane. The grouting could be dusted with powdered rock to make it less obvious, ensuring the cracks between the rocks are kept as small as possible. Where there are deep clefts these can be filled with gravels or clay and used for plants, such as mosses.

A waterfall that exploits a difference in levels is good. The pump needed for this only becomes expensive when a large mass of water has to be carried over a considerable difference in levels.

Photos: Stefan Lehnert – Bioteich

Cascading Waterfall: Interrupted Flow

By using an uneven spill stone that is wider at the bottom than it is at the top, it is possible to create a cascading waterfall, rather than an unbroken curtain of water. A cascade can be created by using several rocks, each set back slightly from the one below, so the water spills down in an uneven way.

Spillways: Curtain Of Water – Unbroken Flow

Here, the spill stone projects outwards over the fall to produce an unbroken curtain of water. A wide stone set only just below the water level so that a broad film of brimming water is produced is most attractive. Few natural stones jut out this way, so a foundation stone is usually used, with a flat stone mortared on top and overhanging it.

ACTION

Excavate the ground according to the design by machine if possible. Hand trim.

Dig out areas for large boulders by hand.

Compact ground and ensure no sharp objects protrude. Cover the ground with sand 50mm deep if necessary.

Cut the underliner to shape and lay over the ground double thickness.

Lay the liner beginning at the lowest section of the stream bed, overlapping by 150mm on the downhill side.

Place additional underliner where boulders and rocks are to be located.

Pour a concrete bed if the boulders and rocks are very large. Thickness will depend on their weight and in certain circumstances reinforcement may need to be included. Grout the waterfall rocks when they are in their final position using a waterproof mix of sand and cement or self-expanding polyurethane.

Ensure cracks between the rocks are kept as small as possible. Dust grout with powdered rock.

Allow spaces for plants and fill with substrate/soil mix.

NOTES

Waterfalls can deplete carbon dioxide levels in the pool, which may affect the biological balance. Fast moving water can also create conditions for algae growth. Nutrient molecules can be absorbed more easily by algae.

Moving Water

Pumping water through tubing (to a waterfall, for example) adds resistance. Allow for friction loss inside the tubing by adding about one metre of head for every 30 metres of horizontal running tube.

Add an allowance for friction loss to the vertical distance that you will be pumping the water. The vertical distance (lift) is measured from the surface of the pool to the top of the waterfall. The resulting sum will be the 'total head' that the pump will be required to pump. You should compare the amount of flow that you require to the flow rate that the pump provides at this specific head.

Example: Figure Head

The vertical distance between the pond's surface level and the top of the waterfall is 900mm and you have 9m of tubing between the pump and the waterfall, so your total head is 1,200mm (300mm per 10.0m + 900mm vertical). If you have a bunch of valves and elbows add 600 or 900mm more to the total head/ lift height. Always check with the pump manufacturer if there is any doubt about the pump's performance at a specific head or pumping height.

ROCKS & BOULDERS

Rocks or boulders should be set in position to achieve a natural look and for best effect resemble natural outcrops. They need to be placed on a concrete ledge in a pond of the same construction and on a concrete raft on top of a liner.

In both cases, the rocks should be placed so that the water level is at least one-third to half of their height. They will need to be bedded on soft mortar or on gravel and soil, depending on their weight and size. Place gravel or mortar behind the boulder where they meet the ground and ensure that, in the case of a liner, it is above the water level and is protected from any damage.

The art of ensuring a natural appearance is to emulate nature and select rocks that are indigenous to the area. To bring rocks from long distances is not only expensive, but damaging to the environment. Many limestone features have been damaged by the removal of rocks and the use of artificial rocks (as seen at the Welsh Green Festival) and may well have to be considered in the future.

Stepping Stones

Although especially suitable for informal pools, stepping stones can be incorporated into formal ones, where squares of stone or paving slabs used for the surrounds can be continued across

Photo: Fairwater Ltd – Bionova

the water. They need not follow a straight course or be of the same size.

Except in shallow water, set the stepping stones on raised supports adjusted to the water level. Make sure the base of the pool is firm and well compacted, protecting the liner with several layers of underlay material. Build the stone or brick supports on a series of concrete footings or a continuous strip of concrete to spread the load and provide stability. Place the stepping stones on a mortar bed on the supports, checking for perfect levels, as this is critical.

STEPS & LADDERS

STEPS

The two main components of steps are risers and treads, and their size plays a significant part in their overall appearance. External steps can be far more generous in size than those inside a building, but they should have a rise between 80–170mm. The outdoor scale makes the use of any formula for calculating the size of risers and treads extremely difficult. Single steps used in isolation are dangerous, as they are easily overlooked.

Treads

These should not be less than 350mm, their width not being less than the going (depth). Non-slip materials are preferable. Where slab treads are used they should overhang the risers by 15mm.

Risers

These should be well marked, especially where the material used is different from the treads.

Photo: Woodhouse Natural Pools Ltd

Photo: Woodhouse Natural Pools Ltd

Photo: Stefan Lehnert – Bioteich

Handrails

If extensive use by elderly people is anticipated, or if the vertical drop at the side of the steps exceeds 600mm, a hand rail should be included. Reference should also be made to building regulations.

Construction

Most flights of steps usually involve the use of a concrete structure, possibly with mesh reinforcement. In most cases it will be possible to cast the concrete in situ as a continuous mass element. The use of reinforcement is recommended in all but the most stable of ground to guard against any differential movement. When flights of steps are flanked by retaining walls the overall appearance, as well as the structural stability, will be better if the steps are built into the walls. This is especially important if the ground has been backfilled and there is some danger of movement.

If timber is used for the construction of steps beware that it can swell under water and may even become twisted or warped. Also any screws used can be snapped and damaged.

Some contractors are now using sub-frames of steel and have it galvanised. This is then clad with timber that in some cases can be thinner. For angled steps made by bolting steel to steel there is no need for concrete balance weights.

LADDERS

There are two types of ladders. The first is made of stainless steel—approximately 40–50mm round section—which has a curved top with three treads. It is secured to a timber deck or paved surface using bolts and anchors.

The second type is made of hardwood timber and the components are screwed together. This is also bolted to the deck.

EDGES

Next to the perimeter wall drain there are many opportunities to have an edge in keeping with the surroundings of the garden or landscape.

If mown grass is desired then a hard edge will be necessary to contain the grass and allow for mowing.

There are various materials available for visible edges, such as stone, brick, timber, and rock. Ideally, the selection of material should be based on what is appropriate for that area or region. Stone should be cut into rough square or rectangular pieces to ensure the retention of a natural appearance. Fairly large pieces can be used for edging without the use of mortar on the same principle

Photo: Dürig Gartenbau

as dry stone wall. Where more precise cut stone has been used in surrounding buildings and landscape, it would be preferable to emulate this if the edge is visible above or below the water line.

There are many examples of various edges available, especially ones where gravel, pebbles, and shingle can be used. The slope to ensure their containment has to be shallow and this type of edging offers a textured contrast with the water, as well as offering a gradual transition from dry ground to water.

For small children, the cobble beach is a small deterrent for access to the water due to its uneven surface.

Photo: Woodhouse Natural Pools Ltd

Photos: Stefan Lehnert – Bioteich

DECKING

For full technical information on decks, boardwalks, bridges, pergolas, etc., readers are referred to *Landscape Detailing Volume 3 'Structures'*.

However, I have included construction details for a simple deck, jetty, bridge, and boardwalk that will be in keeping with a natural swimming pool. See Chapter 10.

ACTION

To make the water appear to run well back beneath the decking it is important not to position it too high above the water level.

Construction of low level decks is the easiest to undertake by the self builder. High level decks or decks on sloping ground should be undertaken by a professional builder.

In areas where children are likely to play a shallow ledge could be incorporated beneath the decking that can double as a planting area. This will act as a safety device, as any child stepping off the deck would only be in ankle deep water among the rushes and plants.

The construction consists of support posts, bearers, joists, and surface boards.

The size of the posts should be 100 × 100mm (4 × 4 in) or 150 × 150mm (6 × 6 in), depending on the distance being spanned by the bearer timbers. These should be 75 × 100mm (3 × 4 in) or 100 × 150mm (4 × 6 in). Joists in some circumstances may not be necessary, such as thicker surface boards, but are usually 75 × 50mm (3

Photo: Stefan Lehnert – Bioteich

× 2 in), depending on the span. The surface boards should be 50 × 100mm (2 × 4 in) or 50 × 150mm (2 × 6 in), with chamfered edges for a neat finish.

Support posts in water can be set into concrete footings, and in some cases into hollow pipes that are set into the footings. This makes it easier to replace the posts in the future. The concrete footings are at least 600 × 600 × 600mm (2 × 2 × 2ft) and are built on several layers of underliner.

The support posts can be fixed to the footings with a 25mm (1in) reinforcing rod used as a dowel. The posts must not be more than 1.80m (6ft) apart and the bearers or beams more than 1.0–1.20m (3-4ft) apart, with joists approximately 600mm (2ft) centres. The bearers should be either coach bolted to the sides of the posts or nailed on top of the posts using galvanised hardware.

The surface boards can be either screwed or nailed to the joists or the bearers with a 10mm (3/8in) gap. Ensure screws or nails are countersunk. The boards should overhang bearers by at least 75mm (3") on all sides, except where the deck is required to extend over the water far more to create a better visual effect.

The timber for decking should be a high quality hardwood and have the ability to withstand being cleaned by a power sprayer or wire brush to remove dirt, moss, etc. Softwoods will not last as long, and if used care has to be taken that they have not been chemically treated. It is preferable for the builder to apply a product that is known to be safe for people and wildlife.

Some sanding or planing may be necessary on hardwood timber—such as rough hewn oak—to remove splinters.

Photos: Richard Weisler – Wassergarten

JETTIES & BOARDWALKS

JETTIES

Jetties or landing stages can be considered open-ended bridges that provide access from dry land to the water where a small boat can come alongside. They can make an attractive feature. The pool must be reasonably large to begin with; anything less than 175 square metres would not accommodate one comfortably.

Their construction is similar to a wooden bridge.

Posts: set in pairs at intervals and bridged by bearers that support the cross surface boards. The distance apart for the posts depends on the length of the bearers and the load it has to carry, but a span of 1.80-2.40m (6-8ft) is a reasonable length. The surface boards should have a gap between them to prevent water from collecting as described under Decking.

The height of the jetty should always ensure that bearers are above the water. The width can vary according to its use and to some extent it should be

Photo: Anglo Swimming Ponds

in proportion to its length. However, it should not be less than 900mm (3ft) wide.

The main cross members can be jointed and bolted through using galvanised hardware. It is worthwhile leaving one post at the end taller than the rest by 600-800mm (24-32") to serve as a mooring post that can add to the overall visual appearance.

BOARDWALKS

These are generally used to provide safe access across marshy or boggy ground or sand dunes. They are best built of timber and have a foundation framing and decking; if over 750mm (2'6") above the ground then a handrail is required.

Depending on location and design, the foundation is always a pier or wood post, and if in contact with water and a softwood is used it will need to be treated with a non-toxic preservative.

Construction is similar to jetties and flat bridges and the surface boards play the same important structural role.

Elements made of wood

The following considerations must be taken into account when using wood:

Surface structure

Wood strength classification

Finish of the wood

Bleeding and resin bleeding

Wood protection: wood preservatives must not give off any substances that are harmful to human health and/or adversely affect the biology of the natural pool

Non-slip surface during use

Fastening materials must be durable and corrosion-free

BRIDGES

To make them practical and safe to use bridges should be at least 600mm (24") wide—depending on the size of the project even wider. Always ensure the ends of a bridge are flush with any paving to avoid tripping.

Sometimes it may be necessary to add a handrail; these should be at least 900mm high (36"). If possible, try to merge the ends of the rails into any areas of plants, rather than coming to an abrupt stop.

The maximum span of an unsupported bridge is 2.40 metres (8ft)—wider ones will need additional supports.

Timber bridges will require far more maintenance than bridges made of stone, brick, metal, or concrete. Ensure they do not become slippery when wet by using fine wire mesh or a grit in an epoxy resin on the surface.

Bridges can also be purchased ready made, but check the requirements for the foundation and fixing.

The construction of a simple flat bridge can follow the same method given for the jetty.

Photo: Michael Littlewood

Photo: Brian Morse

Photo: Jeff Knox

Photo: Richard Weixler

BEACHES

Beaches are not only visually appealing, but allow for gentle access to the pool for people and wildlife. Beaches can be made of shingle, graded pebbles, or cobblestones; these materials should be sourced from your local area if at all possible.

A simple gentle sloping shingle beach is an inexpensive and easy to install feature. Only smooth washed shingle should be used, as sharp stones could damage the liner. Ensure the shingle is laid on an underliner to protect the main rubber frame.

Press some mortar along the beach edge to stop any shingle from slipping into deeper water.

Graded rounded pebbles can make a natural covering for a shallow beach, especially in colours that match any local stone colours. Grade the stones using the smallest nearest the water.

Cobblestones come in a variety of sizes, but for the best effect use those that are a minimum of 50mm, going up to around 150mm.

Photo: Stefan Lehnert – Bioteich

Photo: Fairwater Ltd – Bionova

Photo: Stefan Lehnert – Bioteich

7

WATER

TESTING

Photo: Stefan Lehnert – Bioteich

At some time during the project and before completion of construction the water should be tested. It is very important to know the chemical composition and pH. This can be obtained from your domestic water supply company. You can ask a private laboratory to conduct an analysis for you. Alternatively, you can purchase a test kit and do it yourself.

When taking water samples, make sure the container is well rinsed in the same water that it is filled with to overflowing.

Also ensure it contains no air, as this may allow contamination. Wrap the lid of the container with 'duck' tape to ensure it is completely sealed.

Nitrate

A Nitrate test kit is now available from Viresco (UK) Ltd. It is very easy to use and consists of ten foil wrapped dip strips and a simple colour chart. It is packed in a flat plastic bag. It also indicates the presence of nitrite, allowing detailed checking of water quality.

NOTE

Phosphates do not appear on many utility company tests so a separate test will be necessary. Phosphates are added to domestic water supplies which, while having no effect on humans, cause considerable problems with algae in natural swimming ponds.

Be aware that well water usually contains iron and special care is necessary.

REQUEST

Natural Swimming Pool Water Analysis

EVALUATION BY

Private Company...

Project name:...

Water taken from (well, natural or main water supply etc):...

ANALYSIS

Bacteriology: (only necessary if the filling water is not used for drinking water)

Psychrophilic germs (colony forming units/ml, 22°C):...

Fecal coliforms (colony forming units/100 ml):..

Fecal streptococci (colony forming units/100 ml):...

Chemistry:

pH Value:..

Conductivity (_S/cm):...

Ammonium (mg/1 NH4):..

Nitrate (mg/1 NO3):...

Carbonate hardness (°dKH - degrees of carbonate hardness from the German system):

....

Total phosphorous (exact to the microgram P per litre!) (μg/1 P):...................................

Potassium permanganate consumption (mg/1):..

Data of the Planned Natural Pool

Total water surface (m2):...

Total water volume (m3):...

RESULT

The above filling water is

☐   Suitable

☐   Requires treatment to make it suitable

☐   Not suitable

Signature...

Company...

Date...

121

ANALYSIS

The water test should reveal a complete analysis, showing if any corrections need to be made to various elements.

Aims

The pH of the pool should be between 6.4 and 7.6.

The concentration of nitrate (NO_2) should be less than 0.1ppm.

Phosphate levels should not exceed 10ug/1 litre.

At a pH of 6.4 to 7.2 and 3 to 8 KH (carbonate hardness), the CO_2 concentration should be between 5 to 15 ppm.

Carbonate hardness (part of water hardness) should be 3 to 8 KH.

A pH value that is too low can be raised with the addition of chalk fertiliser and highly organic aids, such as citric acid, formic acid, and hydrochloric acid.

The water should be clear and clean, as well as iron and sulphur free.

aes analytical and environmental services   **Analytical Report**

Analytical & Environmental Services, Northumberland Dock Road, Wallsend, Tyne and Wear. NE28 0QD
Tel: 01912968500 Fax: 0191 2968560 www.aes-labs.co.uk

1181

| Client: | John Fulton | Address: | Total Soultions Direct LTD 44 The Green |
| | Miscellaneous Private analysis | | Hurworth Darlington |

Contract Ref.:	SPRINGS-3556	Postcode:	DL2 2AA
Contract Description:	Well Analysis		
AES Project Manager:	Jane Anderson		

| Lab No.: | 1796129 | Sample Name: | TOTAL SOLUTIONS DIRECT SAMPLE |
| Date & Time Taken: | 30/11/07 00:00 | Date Received: | 30/11/07 |

SAMPLED BY CLIENT / NO3,NO2 & NH4 none accredited   Date Started: 30/11/07
Collected From: TOTAL SOLUTIONS DIRECT, 44 THE GREEN, HURWORTH, DARLINGTON

PARAMETER	RESULT	METHOD	SITE	
* non-coliforms at 37C	>100 /100ml	HY-001	HY	
presumptive coliforms	26 /100ml	HY-001	HY	
total coliforms	26 /100ml	HY-001	HY	
* non-coliforms at 44C	0 /100ml	HY-002	HY	
presumptive E.coli	0 /100ml	HY-002	HY	
total E.coli	0 /100ml	HY-002	HY	
22C plate count	>300 /ml	HY-003	HY	#
37C plate count	>300 /ml	HY-003	HY	#
colour	3.6 mg/l Pt/Co scale	HY-201	HY	
conductivity	810 uS/cm @20C	HY-201	HY	
pH	7.5 pH units	HY-201	HY	
turbidity	1.0 NTU	HY-201	HY	
ammonium	<0.026 mg/l NH4	HY-207	HY	
nitrate	76 mg/l NO3	HY-207	HY	
nitrite	<0.0024 mg/l NO2	HY-207	HY	
aluminium	25 ug/l Al	HY-251	HY	
iron	37 ug/l Fe	HY-251	HY	
manganese	2.7 ug/l Mn	HY-251	HY	
phosphorus total	1600 ug/l P	HY-251	HY	
copper	<0.00064 mg/l Cu	HY-256	HY	
lead	<0.025 ug/l Pb	HY-256	HY	
zinc	<0.54 ug/l Zn	HY-256	HY	

ELEMENTS

Hardness

Calcium is the most important mineral in water, and it is often combined with others. $CaCO_3$ (calcium carbonate) dissolves in water. The higher amounts there are, the harder the water. The CaO contained in calcium carbonate can be measured to produce a value of measurement: the degree of hardness. 1 degree = 0.01g of CaO per litre of water. The scale ranges from 0-30 degrees of hardness (^{o}dH):

Very soft   = 0 to 4 ^{o}dH
Soft   = 4 to 8 ^{o}dH
Medium hard   = 8 to 12 ^{o}dH
Rather hard   = 12 to 18 ^{o}dH
Hard   = 18 to 30 ^{o}dH
Very hard   = >30 ^{o}dH

Test kits to establish these values can be purchased. The total hardness of the water depends on its origin. Tap water, well water, and groundwater may have considerably different degrees of hardness.

Ideally, the water should have GH values ranging from 'soft' to 'rather hard' (between 4 and 18 ^{o}dH). If not, thin the water and lower hardness by adding rainwater.

PH values

Plants require small amounts of calcium and also magnesium (a trace element). Calcium, in the form of calcium carbonate, also influences the pH value, indicating acidity. The scale range is from 0-14, where a value under 7 is acidic and a value over 7 is alkaline. The value of 7 is neutral, meaning acidic and alkaline values are evenly balanced. For plant growth a pH value of 6-7 (slightly acidic) is favourable. When calcium molecules bind with water molecules the pH value of the water rises and it becomes more alkaline. Stones, gravel, or sand, for example, can introduce calcium to the water. On the other hand bacteria can release acids from decaying plants, so the pH value will never remain constant.

Nitrates

Nitrogen is also present in the water and combines with other elements. Nitrate is formed, which is the best way for plants to absorb nitrogen. It encourages the growth of algae. Once the algae have absorbed the nitrates in the water—which happens quickly when the water warms up—they die off just as quickly. The aerobic bacteria consume large quantities of oxygen breaking the dead algae down, which can lead to an acute shortage and kill life in the pool.

Algae quickly spreads in water rich in nutrients that has been warmed by the sun. When they form dense masses they should be removed and shade provided, and floating plants should be introduced.

Due to the overfertilisation of agricultural land, large amounts of nitrate are increasingly found in groundwater. Concentrations of up to 200mg per litre are no rarity. Excessive concentrations of nitrate may gradually reduce the effectiveness of the pool's filter system (plants consume nitrate). Ideally, the swimming pool should not contain more than 10mg of nitrate per litre.

Photo: Stefan Lehnert – Bioteich

Phosphates

Phosphates (PO₄) also encourage algae growth. If there is an increase in phosphates and algae take over (green water) radical measures are necessary, such as aerating the pool or changing the water with a thorough cleansing. There are products that deal with algae, but these are only a temporary solution if the causes are not identified and removed.

Phosphates are often added to potable water to provide correction from corrosion; tap water may often contain high concentrations of phosphate.

Ideal value: < 0.01mg per litre

Biologically, phosphates cannot be filtered out sufficiently. Reduce phosphate concentrations in the filler water by adding suitable phosphate binders, or through the use of phosphate strippers supplied by some companies.

Oxygen and Carbon Dioxide (O2 and CO2)

Oxygen is present in water in a dissolved state and the amount that water can absorb is temperature dependent. As temperatures increase the maximum amount of oxygen that will dissolve in water decreases. Conversely, cooler water holds more oxygen. During the summer when ambient temperatures rise this can have a critical effect.

The primary source of oxygen in the pool water is at the surface, where it contacts the surrounding air. If the water in pools is heavily stocked with floating plants they may be seriously deprived of oxygen exchange and additional aeration will be required.

Oxygen levels are increased through the effects of waterfalls, streams, bubble fountains, etc., that provide aeration. In some instances supplying air via an air pump can also increase the necessary oxygen.

It is important to have sufficient submerged and oxygenating plants, as they will add oxygen during the daytime and not deplete it drastically at night. Generally one or two bunches of these plants per square metre will be adequate to balance photosynthesis and respiration.

While excess carbon dioxide in water can affect the pH, it can also indicate a shortage of oxygen. The remedy is aeration.

Rain or tap-water

Rainwater from the roofs of buildings is soft water and mostly free from harmful substances; it can be used to top up a pool. However, it is advisable to ensure a filter is incorporated into the downpipe or the storage tank if one is used.

The usual source for the pool is tap water, which can be costly, but not everyone has the means to collect enough rainwater or has their own well.

Depending on the region, even tap water can vary in quality (hardness, pH value, and calcium content). Chlorine is added to it and there are also agricultural impurities and pesticides that can not be completely removed. Rainwater is soft water without the mineral calcium. Plants thrive when watered with rainwater.

Source: Reference 1

Biological balance

In a natural swimming pool the right biological conditions are created so that there is a natural balance in the water.

In the pool, water movement is encouraged by the shallow water zones that slope gently into the deeper waters of the pool. The shallow areas warm up more quickly than the deeper ones and offer various microorganisms different living conditions in the cooler and deeper areas. Cool and warmer waters inter-mix. In addition, the plants in the pool that have been chosen specifically for their locations also increase the variety of micro-planktons in the water.

How the balance is established

Underwater plants take their food directly from the water, taking up nitrates and phosphates and leaving less for algae. One form of algae (*Chara aspera*) removes calcium from the water. It can be placed on the floor of the pool. Another effective underwater plant is *Ceratophyllum demersum*.

Floating plants, such as *Hydrocharis morsus-ranae* and *Stratiotes aloides*, also take their food directly from the water. As they provide shade, they contribute to the prevention of algae build-up. When there are no excess nutrients in the water a balance has been established. The water can cloud over occasionally, but if algae appear regularly it is a sign there are excess nutrients in the water.

For more detailed information see 'Biology' in Section 3 of Natural Swimming Pools – Inspiration for Harmony with Nature

QUALITY

Water Plants

Water plants influence water quality in numerous ways:

They increase the inner surface of the body of water and form large surfaces for bacteria, algae, and animal organisms to develop, thus increasing biochemical turnover.

During the day plants release oxygen directly into the water through photosynthesis. Then, during the night, part of this oxygen is utilized again by the plants themselves.

Water plants can bind nutrients that enter the water to a considerable extent. They turn them into organic substance (bio-mass) and eliminate them from the nutrient cycle for a longer period. Underwater plants directly compete with algae for nutrients.

Water plants have an impact on almost all chemical values and serve water quality by acting as a buffer, controlling negative influences.

The earth in which water plants grow also has an important influence on water quality. Here the demands made on the earth seem to be a paradox: On one hand, the earth should be rich in nutrients so that water plants thrive, while at the same time it should be weak in nutrients to prevent the growth of algae. Yet in a natural pond the earth itself can fulfil these demands.

No earth rich in nutrients should be in direct contact with the water. It should be covered by the substrate, making the nutrients available only to the roots of desirable plants. However, water plants will thrive solely in gravel.

WATER LOSS

The water level must not drop below the minimum level required for the particular type of natural pool, as damage to the system is likely to result (e.g., poor flow through the regeneration area, pump damage).

Even in a correctly installed pool there will be certain water losses caused by normal use and splashing, but particularly also due to evaporation:

direct evaporation (due to sun, wind, low relative humidity of the air, etc., even under frost/icy conditions); this is significantly increased by movement of the water (e.g., due to brooks, fountains, or water features);

indirect evaporation via plants;

via stones and stone mounds that protrude from the water.

On average, the water loss due to evaporation is around 2mm per day, but if conditions are right it can also be as high as 12mm per day—this corresponds to 12 litres per square metre of water surface area. In addition, this loss can be increased to more than 20mm due to use of the pool and splashing.

If these losses are not balanced by natural precipitation, the pool system will need to be refilled—notes about 'top up' water can be found in chapter 4, Plumbing.

When water is lost, it is easy to assume the worst—a hole in the liner. Often other causes are found:

The pump fittings are not tight.

Valves or ball taps are dripping.

The overflow has been placed too low.

A deep-lying fold on the edge of the pool is letting water escape.

Water is running out of the sides of a stream or waterfall.

Water is running along a pipe intended for an electricity cable and is escaping.

Underliner was laid over the capillary barrier and is sucking the water out.

Leaks

There are ways of finding a hole in the liner without removing all the water and clearing everything. Some firms pump gas under the liner to find the hole. It is also possible to use electro-sound.

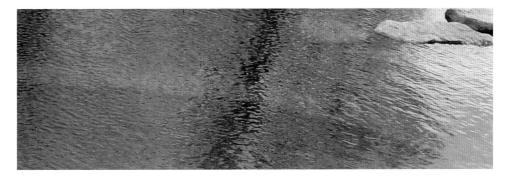

RESERVOIR

Depending on the hydraulic layout of the natural pool, it may be necessary to incorporate a water reservoir. This:

maintains the water level required to keep up the flow over fixed overflow weirs;

provides intermediate storage capacity, allowing the feed to the regeneration area to be carefully controlled;

serves as a water depot that is used to compensate for evaporation losses.

The water reservoir should be dimensional according to the surface area of water so that:

a 1cm water overflow is possible in the swimming area of a single area system;

water losses due to evaporation, use of the pool, and splashing can be compensated.

The volume of the water reservoir can be calculated as follows based on the assumption of a water loss of 8mm per day due to evaporation:

Total water surface area in m^2 × 1 cm +

[(total water surface area in m^2 × 0.8 cm) × no of days without replenishment].

NOTE:

If an automatic feed system for water replenishment is installed, only the overflow height of 1 cm plus water displaced by the swimmers needs to be provided.

Photo: Stefan Lehnert – Bioteich

MOVEMENT

It is a common mistake that *the greater the amount and the faster the water is circulated, the better it will be purified*. The opposite is the case: organisms that purify water need time to complete the process, otherwise water quality can deteriorate.

Another widespread belief is that it is necessary to enrich the oxygen content. First, clear pools are hardly ever low in oxygen. Second, if you introduce more oxygen to the water you will remove carbon dioxide, thereby increasing pH values and harming plants. Even streams and waterfalls can have these effects if their dimensions are not correct.

Many pump manufacturers provide tables to calculate flow rates.

8

PLANTING

GENERAL

The power of plants to purify water has been known for many years; the main example over the last twenty-five years has been the cleaning of human wastes through a reed bed system.

Aerobic bacteria, which require oxygen, and anaerobic bacteria, which do not, are found around plant roots. Both types of micro-organisms work together and break down plant and animal remains, as well as harmful chemical reactions. The roots of these plants have access to the substances released in the process and absorb them as nutrients. Some will escape into the atmosphere as gas.

Some underwater and floating plants cleanse the water more directly. They take nitrates and phosphates from the water and deprive the algae of these two nutrients. They also provide shade and reduce the amount of ultraviolet light that reaches deeper water, thus depriving the algae of this as well.

Water plants are essential and they keep the pH neutral. Through their roots plants release oxygen that kills harmful micro-organisms such as *salmonella*, *coli* bacteria, and *enterococcus*. They also remove harmful environmental substances. They are not just decorative for the natural swimming pool, though their aesthetic value cannot be overlooked. They should be planted in groups that complement each other.

REED BEDS

For many years reed beds have been used for cleaning human wastes and they have proved a highly successful natural system for both public and private properties. They have also been used for the removal of chemicals from polluted water.

Public natural swimming pools in Europe have also found the use of a separate reed bed beneficial and effective in cleaning water.

It is well worth consideration in the UK for private natural swimming pools, especially where the main water supply contains high levels of phosphates. Rain water harvested from roofs could also be cleaned by passing it through a reed bed and then stored for topping up the pool.

The principle for a reed bed system is to use three ponds of varying sizes and depths, allowing the soiled water to pass slowly through each one. As the natural swimming pool uses one or two areas for plants it is relatively easy to add a third for the reeds that will ensure even better clean water.

Particles in the water settle among the plants and these can break down harmful compounds and clean the water. With their vigorous root growth they can aerate the substrate and provide aerobic bacteria with ideal conditions and help keep the pH value neutral. The bacteria turn the particles and harmful compounds into minerals so that the nitrates and phosphates can be absorbed by the plants. Through their roots the plants release oxygen that kills harmful micro-organisms and removes harmful substances.

To be effective the water should pass slowly through each of the plant zones.

Plants suggested for the reed bed area are small and narrow leaved bulrushes, such as *Typha latifolia* and *Typha angustifolia*. *Iris pseudacorus*, *Scirpus lacustris*, *Juncus effuses*, and *Sparganium erectum* could also be added.

Do not use *Phragmites australis*, as it is very rampant and would cause problems, even damaging the liner in some cases. It could be grown in a concrete-lined pool.

A three pond reed bed system could also be used instead of a filter in the swimming pool.

Photo: Stefan Lehnert – Bioteich

LAYOUT

The shoreline of a lake is the model for pool planting. The regeneration zone gradually slopes down into the deeper area. Close to the shore kingcups, marsh irises, reeds, and rushes can be planted, forming the shallow marginal zone. Then come the deeper marginals, such as arrowheads, sweet flag, and sweet grass, followed by the floating and floating leaved plants, like water lilies and floating pond weed. The underwater plants are found both close to the shore and in deeper water.

The regeneration zone will look far more interesting and natural if its depth and width vary, and this will also provide for a greater variety of species. Make sure the width is a minimum of 2m to grade the substrate. Create larger and deeper areas for water lilies to unfold while still allowing the shallow marginals at the water's edge room to spread.

Ensure that plants that tolerate water disturbance are placed at the entrance of the pool or near waterfalls. In shallow water bulrushes are tolerant and in deeper water so is *Ranunculus fluitans*.

As in herbaceous borders, arrange the plants in groups of three, five, or seven. Mirror the groupings in other areas and add larger groupings of seven or nine of the weaker or smaller plants.

DENSITY

Allow for at least an average of four plants per square metre, with a maximum of thirty species: 30% submerged and 70% marginal and floating.

This might break down as follows:

Submerged	7-10 species
Floating	4-6 species
Shallow marginal	5-7 species
Deep marginal	3-5 species

SUB-ZONES

When selecting submerged, marginal, and floating water plants consider the following three main sub-zones:

Shallow water	50–300mm depth
Medium water	300–500mm depth
Deep water	500–750mm depth

These are given as a guide to planting, as after time the plants will send out runners to their ideal location.

Photo: Garten und Schwimmteichbau, N. Sobotta

PLANTS

A list of aquatic plants can be found in my first book *Natural Swimming Pools: Inspiration for Harmony with Nature*, but a second one is included that shows a selection of plants suitable for each of the above three zones.

ACTION

Produce a planting plan and schedule.

Order plants from specialist nurseries.

Let tap water stand for at least forty-eight hours before it comes into contact with plants.

Use plants that can withstand currents in areas of the pool where water flows strongly.

Shade is important, as plants grow better in lower temperatures.

Do not plant too close together.
In two to three years the area will be covered completely.

Don't expect too much growth in the first year, but if growth is poor in the second year it means the nutrient supply in the pool is inadequate.

Apply a mineral fertiliser such as Zeolith over the entire regeneration pool before planting and filling with water.

Sprinkle a biological activator such as Siltex (see page 231) over the water surface once the pool has been filled.

Some varieties of water lilies require shallow water—e.g., the dwarf variety—while others prefer a depth of 1.0 metre or more. If a variety that requires shallow water is planted too deeply it will produce leaves but no flowers. If deep water varieties are planted in shallows their leaves will stick out from the water and not produce any flowers. There are many varieties of water lily available and one can easily be found for any depth of water.

PLANTING DETAILS

In Substrate

All plants must be washed and bare rooted before being planted in the substrate. Move the substrate aside until the underliner is exposed. Plant the roots into fine gravel and then cover with the substrate.

In Baskets

Fill baskets of willow, coconut fibre, or plastic with an appropriate soil medium. After washing plants—including the roots—plant in the basket. Cover the surface with a layer of fine grit or chippings.

Plants in baskets can be kept under better control and are removed much more easily.

CASE STUDY

PLANTING PROPOSALS
FOR A LARGE POOL IN DORSET

showing methodology—water depth zones, size areas, flower colour, planting areas, and plant schedule.

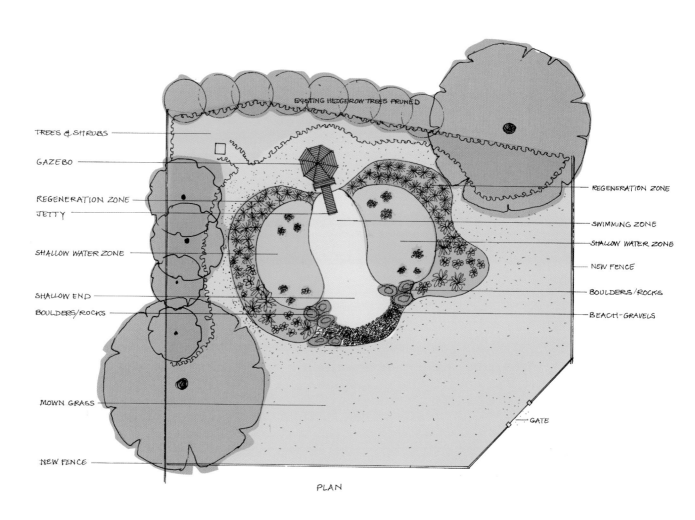

EXISTING HEDGEROW TREES PRUNED

TREES & SHRUBS

GAZEBO

REGENERATION ZONE

JETTY

SHALLOW WATER ZONE

SHALLOW END

BOULDERS/ROCKS

MOWN GRASS

NEW FENCE

REGENERATION ZONE

SWIMMING ZONE

SHALLOW WATER ZONE

NEW FENCE

BOULDERS/ROCKS

BEACH-GRAVELS

GATE

PLAN

PLANTING ZONES

showing planting depth

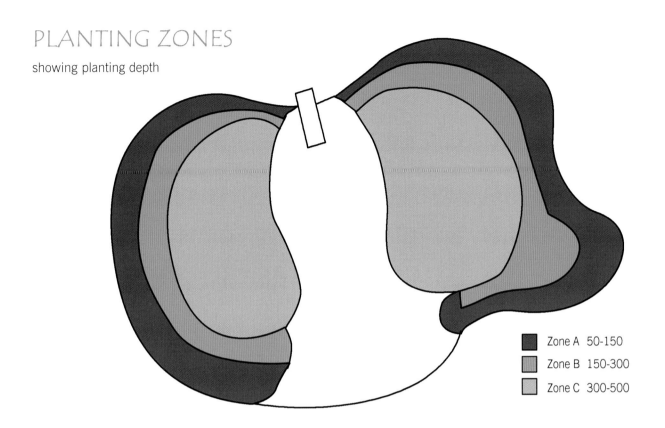

■	Zone A	50-150
■	Zone B	150-300
■	Zone C	300-500

AQUATIC PLANTING

showing size areas

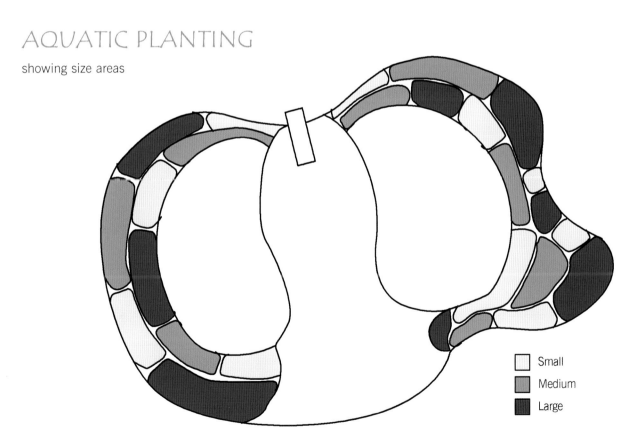

☐	Small
■	Medium
■	Large

FLOWER COLOUR

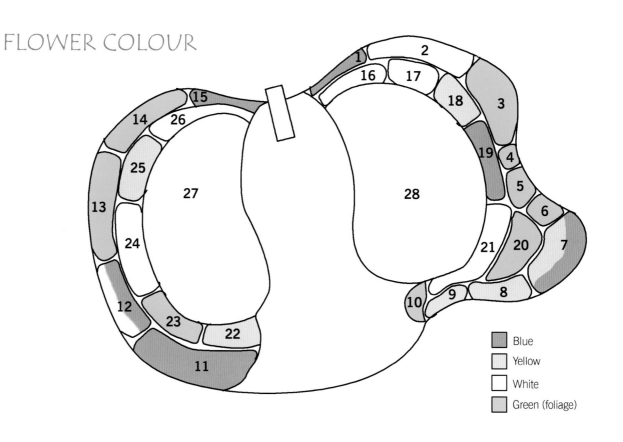

Blue
Yellow
White
Green (foliage)

PLANTING AREAS

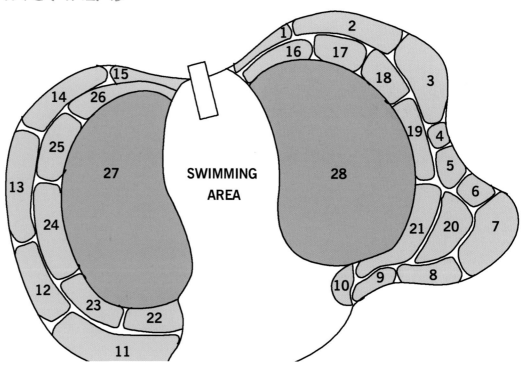

SWIMMING
AREA

AQUATIC PLANT SCHEDULE

Area	Botanical Name	Common Name	Quantity
ZONE A			
1	*Iris versicolor*	Blue Flag	5
2	*Peltrandra undulate*	Green Arrow Arum	12
3	*Typha laxmanii*	Reedmace	15
4	*Juncus effuses spiralis*	Corkscrew Rush	4
5	*Cyperus longus*	Ornamental Rush	3
6	*Juncus effuses spiralis*	Corkscrew Rush	5
7	*Thalia delbata*		10
	Ranunculus lingua	Greater Spearwort	7
8	*Caltha palustris*	Marsh Marigold	11
9	*Iris pseudocorus*	Yellow Flag	5
10	*Typha minima*	Dwarf Reedmace	7
11	*Thalia delbata*		13
	Iris laevigata	Japanese Iris	15
12	*Menyanthes trifoliate*	Bogbean	5
	Myosotis scorpioides	Water Forget me not	5
	Caltha palustris	Marsh Marigold	5
13	*Juncus inflexus*	Hard rush	11
	Glyceria maxima var	Variegated Water Grass	10
14	*Typha laxmanii*	Reedmace	15
15	*Iris versicolor*	Blue Flag	5
ZONE B			
16	*Zantedeschia aethiopica*	Arum Lily	10
17	*Sagittaria latifolia*	American Arrowhead	7
18	*Ranunculus flammula*	Lesser Spearwort	14
19	*Pontederia cordata*	Pickerel Weed	11
20	*Acorus calamus*	Sweet Flag	7
	Butomus umbellatus	Flowering Rush	7
21	*Houttynia cordata Plena*		9
	Carex riperia "Bowles Golden"	Great Pond Sedge	11
22	*Cotula coronpitifolia*	Golden Buttons	5
23	*Calla palustris*	Bog Bean	7
	Carex riperia	Great Pond Sedge	4
24	*Sagittaria latifolia*	American Arrowhead	4
25	*Mimulus luteus*	Monkey Musk	11
26	*Zantedeschia aethiopica*	Arum Lily	7
ZONE C			
27/28	*Aponogeton distchyos*	Water Hawthorn	9
	Nuphar species	Pond Lilies	11
	Nyphoides letata	Water Fringe	5
	Nymphaea species	Water Lilies	25
	Orontium aquaticum	Golden Club	10
SUBMERGED PLANTS			
	Callitriche palustris	Water Starwort	
	Ceratophyllum demersum	Hornwort	
	Chara vulgaris	Stonewort	
	Myriophyllum spicatum	Spiked milfoil	
	Ranunculus aquatilis	Water Crowfoot	

AQUATIC PLANT LIST

SUBMERGED PLANTS

Botanical Name	Common Name	Height	Spread	Water Depth
Callitriche hermaphroditica	Autumnal starwort		60cm24in	5-60cm 2-24in
Callitriche palustris	Water starwort		Indefinite	Shallow or deep water
Callitriche stagnalis	Common water starwort			Up to 1m 3 ft
Callitriche truncata	Short-leaved water starwort		Up to 1m 3ft	
Ceratophyllum submersum	Hornwort		Indefinite	25-50cm 10-60in
Ceratopteris thalictroides	Watersprite		Moderate	
Chara vulgaris	Stonewort		30cm 12in	30cm-3m 1-10ft
Egeria densa			30cm 12in	30-90cm 12-36in
Fontinalis antipyretica	Willowmoss			Up to 2m up to 6ft 6in
Hippuris.vulgaris	Mare's tail, cat's tail, bottle brush, knot grass		15cm 6in	30-90cm 12-36in
Hottonia palustris	Water violet	30-90cm 1-3ft	Indefinite	45cm 18in
Lagarosiphon major, syn.Elodea crispa	Fishweed		Indefinite	1-2m 4ft
Myriophyllum spicatum	Spiked water milfoil		Indefinite	1m 3ft
Myriophyllum verticillatum	Whorled water milfoil		Indefinite	44cm 18in
Potamogeton crispus	Curled pondweed		Indefinite	1m 3ft
Potamogeton pectinatus	Fennel pondweed			50cm- 2.5m 10in -7ft
Ranunculus aquatilis	Water crowfoot		Indefinite	1m 3ft

Flower Colour	Flower Period	Foliage	Position	Comments
		Thin lance shaped in form of bright green rosette	Warm water, dark and shady	Oxygenator
		Pale green foliage	Sun	Oxygenator
			Sun to partial shade	Still or moving water
		Sun to partial shade	Likes still water	
	April-Sept	Dark green leaves	Deep pool conditions sun/shade	Oxygenator
Dense rosettes of feather shaped fronds		Delicate pale green submerged	Sun	Tropical Fern
		Spikes of pale greyish green		Good oxygenator
White		Grey green	Sunny	Good oxygenator
			Sun to partial shade	This very unusual moss can grow in fast-flowing streams, but will survive in a clear pond. It can grow several metres long and is a great oxygenator
		Bright green		
Pale lilac		Bright green ferny leaves	Sun	Slow to establish
	Summer	Reflexed, linear leaves	Sun	Invasive
Tiny red and yellow flowers	Summer	Olive coloured leaves	Sun to partial shade	Good oxygenator, very adaptable prefers clear, alkaline waters
Yellowish flowers		Bright green leaves	Shallow water	Good oxygenator, likes still water
Crimson and creamy white	Summer	Wavy-edged bronze hued leaves	Shade	Needs clear water
			Sun to partial or even full shade	
White buttercup shaped	Summer	Bright to dark green	Deep water	Good oxygenator

FLOATING PLANTS

Botanical Name	Common Name	Height	Spread	Water Depth
Eichhornia crassipes	Water hyacinth		Indefinite	20-30cm 8-12in
Hottonia palustris	Water violet			
Hydrocharis morsus-ranae	Frogbit		10cm 4in	
Lemna.trisulca	Ivy-leaved duckweed		Indefinite	Shallow or deep water
Potamogeton natans	Broad-leaved pondweed			30cm-3m 1ft-10ft
Ranunculus aquatilis	Common water-crowfoot			50cm 20in
Sratiotes aloides	Water soldier	10-20cm4-8in		Indefinite

Flower Colour	Flower Period	Foliage	Position	Comments
Lavendar blue, hyacinth like				Highly invasive Removes chemicals
Delicate mauve	May-June		Sun	When not in flower, can look like a water-milfoil.
Three petalled white flower	July-Aug	Nymphaea-shaped leaves	Full sun, on top or under water	Grows from runners overwintering as buds in mud at the bottom of the pond. Likes still, unpolluted water with high alkalinity.
	May-July	Oval transparent green fronds		Excellent for clearing water
Small green	May-Aug	Both underwater and above-water leaves	Full sun	Needs to be able to reach the surface to produce its flower spike. Prefers still, clear water
Small, white, in profusion	Mar-May		Full sun	Likes still or slow-flowing water, not too fussy about the soil, but is usually found in alkaline rather than acid waters.
Small and white	July-Aug	Spiky cactus-like leaves	Full sun, in shallow water or floating on deeper water	Unusual shape and very adaptable: can grow as free-floating, submerged or rooted, emergent plant. Good oxygenator

FLOATING LEAVED PLANTS

Botanical Name	Common Name	Height	Spread	Water Depth
Aponogeton distachyus	Cape pond weed, water hawthorn		60cm several metres	30cm-1m 1-3ft 3in
Limnorbium spongia	American frogbit			
Nuphar advena	American spatt...			
		23cm 9in	30cm 12in	10-... 4-6in
Nuphar japonica	Japanese pond...	10cm 4in	Indefinite	7cm 3in
Nuphar lutea	Yellow water-lily			
		45-60cm 18-24in	45cm 18in	to 10cm 4in
Nuphar pumila	Brandy bottle	15-60cm 6-24in	Indefinite	to 10cm 4in
Nymphaea Species and varieties	Water lily	60cm-1m 2-3ft	Indefinite	7-10cm 3-4in
		60cm 2ft		5-7cm 2-3in
Nymphaea alba	White Water-lily	60-90cm 2-3ft	less 90cm 3ft	15cm 6in
Nymphaea pygmaea 'Helvola'	MiniatureWater lily	30-70cn (long)		
Nymphoides peltata	Fringed water-lily	90cm 3ft	60cm 2ft	7cm 3in
Orontium aquaticum	Golden club	20cm 30 12-..	Indefinite	to 10cm 4in
			60cm 2ft	25cm 10in
Pistia	Water lettuce	22-30cn 9-12in		7-15cm 3-6in
				15cm 6in

Flower Colour	Flower Period	Foliage	Position	Comments
White	Summer		Full sun	Can take over a pond but is easy to trim and manage
				Low creeping for edges
	Summer	Heart shaped, bright green		
White centred, blue				
Golden yellow	Spring	Rich green leaves		
White with red stems	Spring	Bluish green heart shaped leaves		Spreads quickly
Sky-blue	June and Sept	Sword shape	Moist soil, must not dry out	
Violet blue		Sword shape grey green	Wet soil	
Pale mauve	Summer	Small green, purple, aromatic	Sun or partial shade	Spreads rapidly, plant in a basket
Large, pink	July-Sept		Full sun, on bank or floating	
Greenish purple		Cream edged foliage		
Yellow	Early summer	Sword shape grey green	Sun or partial shade	
Yellow or white	Summer	Arrow shaped, bright green leaves		
Yellow	Late spring	Heart shaped & long stalked		
Violet	Summer	Blue, green with white mealy coating		Tall graceful foliage plant

MARGINAL PLANTS

Botanical Name	Common Name	Height	Spread	Water Depth
SMALL (10-50cm)				
Hypericum elodes	Marsh St John's wort	5-10cm 2-4in	Indefinite	To 10cm 4in
MEDIUM (50-120cm)				
Acorus calamus	Sweet flag	75-90cm 2½-3ft	90cm+ 3ft+	6-25cm 3-10in
Alisma plantago-aquatica	Water plantain	75-90cm 2½-3ft	45cm 18in	15-24cm 6-10in
Caltha palustris	Marsh marigold	45-60cm 18-24in	45cm 18in	to 10cm 4in
Cyperus longus	Ornamental rush	60-90cm 2-3ft	90cm 3ft	5-25cm 2-10in
Peltrandra undulate 'Green Arrow'	Arum	75cm2_ ft	45cm18in	25cm10in
Pontederia cordata	Pickerel weed	75cm 30in	45cm 18in	25-30cm 10-12in
Zantedeschia aethiopica 'Green Goddess'	Arum Lily	60-75cm 24-30in	45-60cm 18-24in	25cm 10in
LARGE (120-200cm)				
Cyperus papyrus	Paper reed	3-5m 10-15ft	1m 3ft	to 25cm 10in
Sagittaria latifolia	American arrowhead, duck potato, wapato	1.5m 5ft	60cm 2ft	30cm 12in
Zantedeschia aethiopica	Arum Lily	75-90cm 30-36in	35-45cm 14-18in	30cm 12in

Flower Colour	Flower Period	Foliage	Position	Comments
Yellow	Summer	Small pale green leaves		
Brown conical flowers	Summer	Iris like, mid green with cream stripes		
Dainty, pinkish white		Oval leaves	Sun or partial shade	A real beauty that can be planted straight into the soil and left alone
Golden yellow	Spring	Rich green leaves		
Red-brown	Late summer	Long, thin, ribbed leaves – dark green		
Soft blue	Late summer	Smooth, narrow, heart shaped leaves		
White splashed greenarum-like with central yellow spike	Summer	Green heart shaped leaves	Sun	Elegant form foliage plant Frost tender
Flower sprays	Summer	Pendulous leaves	Best sheltered from wind	Frost tender
White	Summer	Soft green leaf blades		
White with central green spike	Summer	Dark glossy leaves	Sun	Frost tender

MARGINAL PLANTS

Botanical Name	Common Name	Height	Spread	Water Depth
SMALL (100-500cm)				
Ludwigia palustris	Water purslane	50cm 20in		30cm 12in
MEDIUM (500-1200 cm)				
Sagitaria Sagitifolia	Arrowhead	45-60cm 15-24in	45-65cm	600cm
LARGE (1200-2000cm)				
Sparganium erectum	Branched Bur-reed	150cm 5ft		
Zantedeschia aethiopica	Arum Lily	75-90cm 30-36in	35-45cm 14-18in	30cm- 12in

GRASSES, SEDGES, REEDS & RUSHES

Botanical Name	Common Name	Height	Spread	Water Depth
SMALL (100-500cm)				
Eriophorum angustifolium	Cotton grass	30-45cm 12-18in	Indefinite	5cm 2in
MEDIUM (500-1200 cm)				
Cyperus longus	Ornamental rush	60-90cm 2-3ft	90cm3ft	5-25cm 1-9in
Glyceria fluitans	Floating sweet-grass	25-90cm 9in-3ft		
Glyceria maxima var.variegata	Variegated water grass	60-75cm 2-2_ ft	Indefinite	15cm 6in
Juncus effusus var spiralis	Corkscrew rush	30-60cm 1-2ft	60cm2ft	to 7_cm 3in
Juncus inflexus	Hard rush	55-75cm 22-30in	55cm 21in	0-15cm 0-6in
Typha minima	Dwarf reedmace	30-45cm 12-18in	30cm 12in	
LARGE (1200-2000cm)				
Typha laxmani	Reedmace	90-120cm 3-4ft		15cm 6in

ZONE C – water depth 300-500cm

Flower Colour	Flower Period	Foliage	Position	Comments
Tiny bell shaped	Summer	Suffused	Full sun with purple	
Small, white	July-Aug	Spectacular leaves	Sun	
Green	June-Aug		Sun, in deeper water	Very vigorous, so do not plant in small pond
White with central	Summer	Dark, glossy leaves green spike	Sun	Foliage plant

ZONE A – water depth 50-150cm

Flower Colour	Flower Period	Foliage	Position	Comments
White downy 'cotton balls'	Early summer	Dense tufts of grass-like leaves	Acid conditions, such as peaty soil	
Silvery	May-Aug		Sun	
Heads of greenish spikelets	Summer	Striped with creamy white, often flushed pink at base		
Green-brown	Mid-summer	Leafless stems	Doesn't mind shade	
Dark brown inflorescences	June to August	Bright green grass-like foliage		
		Grass like leaves		

GRASSES, SEDGES, REEDS & RUSHES

Botanical Name	Common Name	Height	Spread	Water Depth
SMALL (100-500cm)				
Carex riparia 'Bowles Golden'		30-50cm 12-20in	50cm 20in	5-20cm 2-8in
MEDIUM (500-1200 cm)				
Acorus calamus variegatus	Sweet flag	1m 4ft	30cm 12in	
Butomus umbellatus	Flowering rush	1m 4ft	60cm 24in	
Carex riparia	Great pond sedge	90-120cm 3-4ft	1m 40in	0-25cm 0-10in
Glyceria aquatica variegata	Manna grass	1m 3ft 3in	Indefinite	
Juncus effusus	Soft rush	30-120cm 1-4ft	1m 40in	0-25cm 0-10in
Typha latifolia	Reed mace or false bull rush	1-1.20m 3-4ft	1m 3ft3in	25cm 10in
LARGE (1200-2000cm)				
Arundo donax	Giant reed	2.4-5m 8-16ft	3-4m 10-13ft	
Typha angustifolia	Lesser reed mace	1.8-2.1m 6-7ft		60cm 2ft

GRASSES, SEDGES, REEDS & RUSHES

Botanical Name	Common Name	Height	Spread	Water Depth
MEDIUM (500-1200 cm)				
Scirpus lacustris tabernaemontani 'Zebrinus'	Zebra rush	1.2m 4ft	60cm 24in	30cm 12in
LARGE (1200-2000cm)				
Scirpus lacustris	Common bulrush	2.4m 8ft	1m 3ft3in	

ZONE B – water depth 150-300cm

Flower Colour	Flower Period	Foliage	Position	Comments
	May-August			
		Green, cream striped		
Rose pink	Mid-summer	Sword shaped, long and thin		
Brown spikelets	May-June	Coarse leaves		
		Variegated green and cream, grasslike		
Brown inflorescences	June to August	Dark green stems		
Light brown male flowers		Grey-green spiky leaves		
		Long blue-grey leaves	Damp sandy soil, sun	
Huge brown spikes	June-July		Sun	Very vigorous so do not plant in small pond

ZONE C – water depth 300-500cm

Flower Colour	Flower Period	Foliage	Position	Comments
			Shallow water and sun	
			Likes shade	

EDIBLE AQUATIC PLANTS

In case swimmers get hungry, here is a selection

Botanical Name	Common Name	Edible Part
Acorus calamas	Sweet Flag	Rhizome
Aponogeton distachyos	Cape Pondweed	Tubers, seeds
Beckmannia eruciformis		Tubers, seeds
Butomus umbellatus	Flowering Rush	Tubers, seeds
Chrysoplenium alternifolium and C. oppositifolium	Golden Saxifrages	Leaves
Cornus canadensis	Creeping Dogwood	Fruit
Cyperus longus	Galingale	Roots
Glyceria fluitans	Float Grass	Seeds
Gunnera tinctoria	Gunnera	Leaf stalks
Nasturtium officinale	Watercress	Leaves, seeds
Nuphar lutea	Yellow Water Lily	Roots
Nymphaea alba	White Water Lily	Leaves, flowers
Peltandra alba	White Arrow Arum	Rhizome – cooked. Poisonous raw
P. virginica	Green Arrow Arum	Rhizome – cooked. Poisonous raw
Phragmites communis	Common Reed	Roots, seeds
Pontederia cordata	Pickerel Weed	Seeds, leaf stalks
Sagittaria sagittifolia	Arrow Head	Tubers
Samolus valerandi	Brookweed	Leaves
Scirpus lacustris	Bulrush	Roots, shoots
Sparganium erectum	Bur-Reed	Tubers
Trapa natans	Water Chestnut	Seeds
Typha angustifolia	Smaller Reed Mace	Rhizome, young shoots, seeds, pollen, young spikes
T. latifolia	Greater Reed Mace	Rhizome, young shoots, seeds, pollen, young spikes
Vaccinium palustre	Small Cranberry	Fruit, leaves
Zizania acquatica	Wild Rice	Rhizomes, young shoots, stem bases, seeds

DEFICIENCIES

DEFICIENCIES THAT APPEAR IN PLANTS

Element	Biochemical function	Symptoms of deficiencies
CO_2	Cell development	Growth stops - plants covered by algae
Potassium	Essential nutrient	Necrosis, stunted growth
Iron	Numerous porphyrin compounds	Chlorophyll synthesis is prevented Leaves turn yellow
Manganese	Involved in the development of oxygen Enzymes are activated	Similar to iron deficiency Chlorosis
Magnesium	Essential nutrient required in large quantities	Lightened leaf surfaces
Zinc Oxygen	Cofactor of enzymes: alcohol-dehydrogenate main component of all physiological structures of proteins	Chlorosis: leaf development hindered: yellow marks appear on the leaves, leaves turn yellow, plants fail to thrive
Copper	Component of many enzymes; phenolate, ascorbic-oxide	Growth hindered
Molybdenum	Component of enzymes of inorganic nitrogen metabolism	Discoloured leaves, chlorosis, no formation of flowers
Boron	Complex formation of polyhydroxide compounds	Tissue development hindered 'Brittle'

Reference 2 – Source: Richard Weisler

PLANT IMAGES

Plants marked * are native (UK) species
Blue text denotes aquatic plants
Source: Fairwater Ltd

Achillea ptarmica
Sneezewort*

Acorus calamus
Sweet Flag*

Acorus calamus variegatus

Ajuga reptans
Bugle

Alisma plantago-aquatica
Water Plantain*

Aponogeton distachyos
Water Hawthorn*

Arum italicum pictum

Astilbe
Goatsbeard (pink)

Astilbe
Goatsbeard (white)

Athyrium filix-femina
Lady Fern*

Butomus umbellatus
Flowering Rush*

Calla palustris
Bog Arum*

Caltha palustris
Kingcups*

Caltha polypetala
Giant Kingcups

Cardamine pratensis
Cuckoo Flower/Ladies Smock*

Carex morrowii

Carex nigra
Black Sedge*

Carex pendula
Pendulus Sedge*

Carex riparia
Great Pond Sedge*

Carex stricta
Bowles Golden Sedge

Plants marked * are native (UK) species
Blue text denotes aquatic plants

Ceratophyllum demersum – Hornwort*

Cyperus longus
Sweet Galingale*

Dryopteris filix-mas
Male Fern*

Elodea crispa
Curly Pond Weed*

Equisetum japonicum
Japanese Horsetail

Eriophorum angustifolium
Common Cotton-Grass*

Filipendula hexapetala
Dropwort*

Filipendula ulmaria
Meadow Sweet*

Filipendula ulmaria variegata

Filipendula venusta

*Fritillaria meleagris**

Geum rivale
Water Avens*

Glyceria maxima
Reed Sweet Grass*

Glyceria maxima variegata – Green & White Sweet Grass

Gratiola officinalis
Summer Snowflake

Gunnera manicata

Hemerocallis – Day Lily (assorted)

Hosta
Plantain Lily (assorted)

Houtuynia cordata
Orange Peel Plant

Houtuynia cordata
'Harlequin'

Iris ensata
Japanese Clematis Iris

Iris laevigata
Japanese Water Iris

Iris Laevigata variegata

Iris pseudacorus
Yellow Flag Iris*

Iris sibirica
Siberian Iris

Iris versicolor
American Water Iris

Juncus effusus
Soft Rush*

Juncus inflexus
Hard Rush*

Juncus spiralis
Twisted Rush

Libertia grandiflora

Ligularia dentata
'Desdemona'

Ligularia przewalskii
'The Rocket'

Lychnis flos-cuculi
Ragged Robin*

*Lysichiton
Camtschatcensis*
White Skunk Cabbage

Lysimachia nummularia
Creeping Jenny*

*Lysimachia nummularia
aurea* Golden Jenny

Lythrum salicaria Purple
Loosestrife*

Mentha aquatica Water
Mint*

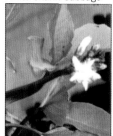
Menyanthes trifoliata
Bogbean*

Mimulus luteus
Yellow Musk*

Myosotis palustris
Water Forget-Me-Not*

Nymphaea
Assorted Water Lilies

Nuphar lutea
Brandy Bottle*

Orontium aquaticum
Golden Club

Phalaris arundinacea picta
Gardeners Garters

Physostegia virginiana
Obedient Plant
(Summer Snow)

Persicaria bistorta
'superba' – Bistort

Pontederia cordata
Pickerel Plant

Primula florindae
Himalayan Cowslip

Primula japonica
Candelabra Primula

Ranunculus aquatilis
Water Crowsfoot*

Ranunculus flammula
Lesser Spearwort*

Ranunculus lingua
Greater Spearwort*

Rumex hydrolapathum
Red Water Dock

Sagittaria sagittifolia
Water Archer*

Salix alba vitellina
Golden Willow

Salix matsudana
'tortuosa' – Twisted
Willow

Saururus cernuus
Swamp Lily/Lizard's Tail

Schizostylis coccinea
Kaffir Lily

Scirpus albescens
Variegated Club Rush

Plants marked * are native (UK) species
Blue text denotes aquatic plants

Scirpus lacustris
Club rush*

Scirpus zebrinus
Zebra Rush

Sparganium erectum
Branched Burr-reed

Sparganium demersum
Unbranched Burr-reed

Thalia dealbata
Mexican Blue Feather

Typha angustifolia
Narrow-leaved
Reedmace*

Typha latifolia
Reedmace*

Typha laxmanii
Golden Headed
Reedmace

Typha minima
Dwarf Reedmace

Veronica beccabunga
Brooklime*

*Zantedeschia
aethiopica*
Arum Lily

PLANT HARDINESS ZONES

USA

Created by the United States Department of Agriculture (USDA), this map is a useful tool for selecting and cultivating plants. The map divides North America into eleven zones based on each region's average minimum winter temperature: Zone 1 is the coldest and Zone 11 the warmest. Locate your Zone, then use that information to select plants that are most likely to thrive in your climate.

ALASKA

Plant Hardiness Zones – USA
Reproduced with permission of the American
Horticultural Society

Range of Average Annual Minimum Temperatures for Each Zone

Zone	Temperature
Zone 1	Below -50° F
Zone 2	-50° to -40° F
Zone 3	-40° to -30° F
Zone 4	-30° to -20° F
Zone 5	-20° to -10° F
Zone 6	-10° to 0° F
Zone 7	10° to 20° F
Zone 8	20° to 30° F
Zone 9	30° to 40° F
Zone 10	40° to 50° F
Zone 11	50° to 60° F

EUROPE

Key to European Countries

AL	Albania
AND	Andorra
A	Austria
B	Belgium
BY	Belorussia
BIH	Bosnia + Hercegovina
BG	Bulgaria
HR	Croatia
CZ	Czech Republic
DK	Denmark
EST	Estonia
FIN	Finland
F	France
MK	Former Yugoslav Republic of Macedonia
D	Germany
GR	Greece
H	Hungary
I	Italy
LV	Latvia
FL	Liechtenstein
LT	Lithuania
L	Luxembourg
M	Malta
MD	Moldavia
MC	Monaco
NL	Netherlands
N	Norway
PL	Poland
P	Portugal
IRL	Republic of Ireland
RO	Romania
RUS	Russian Federation
SK	Slovak Republic
SLO	Slovenia
E	Spain
S	Sweden
CH	Switzerland
TR	Turkey
UA	Ukraine
GB	United Kingdom
YU	Yugoslavia

Average Winter Minimum Temperature

Zones		Celsius	Fahrenheit
Zone 1		below -45	below -50
Zone 2		-45 to -40	-50 to -40
Zone 3		-40 to -34	-40 to -30
Zone 4		-34 to -29	-30 to -20
Zone 5		-29 to -23	-20 to -10
Zone 6		-23 to -18	-10 to 0
Zone 7		-18 to -12	0 to 10
Zone 8		-12 to -7	10 to 20
Zone 9		-7 to -1	20 to 30
Zone 10		-1 to 4	30 to 40
Zone 11		above 4	above 40

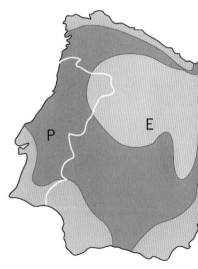

*Plant Hardiness Zones/Europe —
Adapted from* Gardening with Herbs
*by Eric Thomas. Reproduced with kind
permission of the publisher, Collins &
Brown, London.*

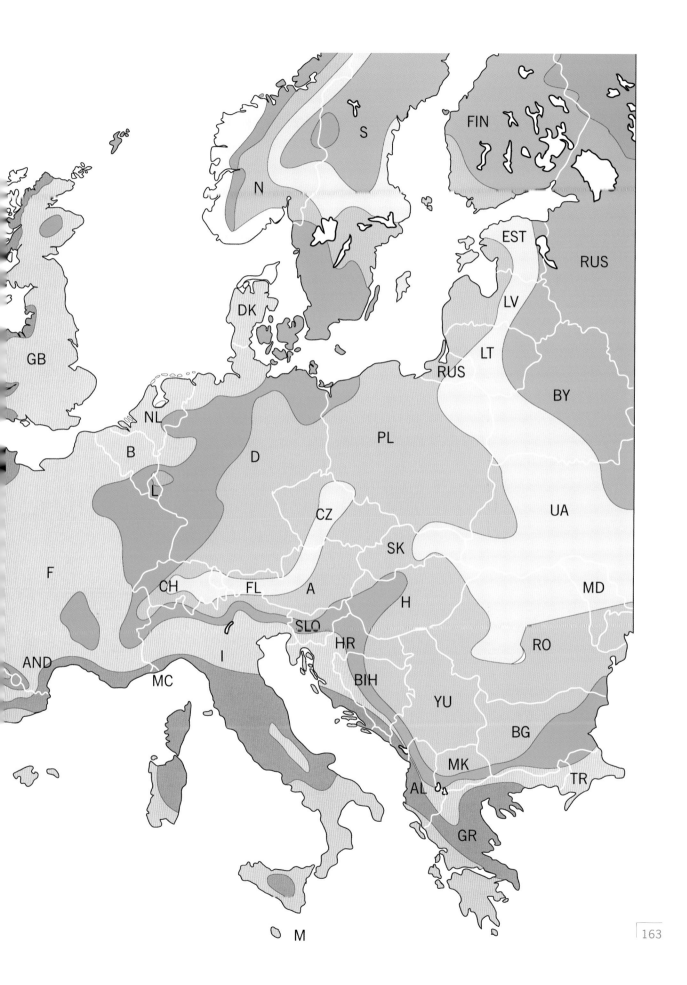

9

CARE

HYGIENE

The importance of hygiene in private natural pools has to be assessed in a similar way to the hygiene requirements in other domestic/private environments. In these areas basic hygiene rules are followed as a matter of course. The following rules apply to natural pools:

Swimmers should have a shower before entering the pool to reduce the amount of dirt, sweat, etc., that is introduced into the pool. The water used must not enter the pool.

Solar powered shower
Photo: Carsten Schmidt

The pool should not be used by persons with contagious diseases, open wounds, or diarrhoea.

Persons with notifiable illnesses must not use the natural pool at all.

Mammals (e.g., dogs, rats, pine martens, badgers, etc.) should be kept away from the water.

Waterfowl should be kept away from the natural pool, as the excrement of these birds may cause hygiene problems. In addition, their behaviour (e.g., diving and searching for food) and the substances they introduce (e.g., nutrients, fish spawn) can have a significantly detrimental effect on the appearance of the natural pool and its ability to function as intended.

Other hygiene risks are presented by the simultaneous presence of snails and waterfowl, as they are among the hosts of certain types of cercariae (cercariae = larva stage of trematode worms or flat worms). Cercariae cause so-called swimming or bathing dermatitis. To prevent cercariae, the following measures should be taken:

Waterfowl should be scared away promptly.

The snail population in the swimming area should be kept as low as possible. In the event of increased infestation the snails must by removed mechanically.

MAINTENANCE

Maintaining your pool in good condition is not an exact science. As you use and enjoy it, experience will show whether you need to adjust the pump's running time or the frequency of cleaning. You will soon develop a regular routine that fits your particular requirements and how often you use the pool. The next few pages offer simple guidelines on how to maintain it.

A natural swimming pool will only work if it is regularly and properly maintained. An inspection and service should be

undertaken in the spring and autumn by the owner or a suitably qualified person or company. The following should be checked:

- Water Transparency

- Pool Edge stability

- Effectiveness of the capillary block

- Exposed liner

- High water losses

- Condition of the liner

- Working condition of the plumbing and electrical systems

- Unusually high levels of algae

- Unusual growth/deficiency symptoms in plants

- It would also be advantageous to have the water tested both for the pool and the top-up supply

Since the pool has no chemical additives and is as natural as any pond it will be attractive to wildlife. You must be prepared to share the environment with the odd frog, newt, or water beetle. These will tend to keep to the regeneration zone and shallow areas since the main swimming area is too deep for them.

Photo: Guido Manzke

first few weeks until the water is clear. The bottom drain can then be purged and the filter cloth changed if used.

Regular Maintenance

DAILY/WEEKLY

• Clear leaves and debris from the skimmer

MONTHLY

• Empty the strainer basket on the circulation pump.

• Check the main filter

• Remove dead leaves from plants in the regeneration zone.

• Purge the bottom drain to remove debris. Vacuum the floor.

ANNUALLY

• Replace the filter cloth if necessary

BIENNIALLY

• Replace the fleece cartridges in the filter if used.

Initial start up

The pool will take some time to establish equilibrium. An algae bloom may develop, especially in the regeneration zone and shallow areas. This is a perfectly normal occurrence and will clear as the higher plants establish themselves. Please bear in mind that the growing season for water plants starts later than the garden. Vigorous growth normally begins during spring, depending on the water temperature.

Any dust and sediment in the water will be gradually filtered out. Using the pool will help by stirring the sediment into suspension so that the filtering process is speeded up. It is recommended to run the circulation pump continuously for the

ALGAE CONTROL

Battling string algae is the hardest part of pool maintenance. Begin treating the water at the first sign of trouble and net out any emerging algae growth. Excessive nitrate and phosphorous in the system will cause problems. Add new oxygenating and floating plants early each spring (they die off in northern climates) and re-apply bacteria.

Be aware that 1g of phosphorous is responsible for 1000g of algae. Algae consume a lot of CO_2, which is the most important plant nutrient, and as a result the pH value can rise so much in the course of a day that other plants are harmed.

If algae are clouding the water, the cause must be established and the situation rectified. It is usually caused by the introduction of too many nutrients linked to a shortage of zoo plankton and competition with underwater plants.

Control

In the transitional phase—spring and autumn—problems can arise caused by too many nutrients. Zeolith is a biologically effective means of dealing with the problem. The granules are added in a quantity of 4 kilos per cubic metre spread out on jute mats or in tubes, or 1-2 kilos per square metre is worked into the plant layer of the pool.

It binds nutrients and encourages bacterial activity; phosphorous, nitrogen, potassium, dissolved heavy metal compounds, etc., are removed and the water becomes clear.

The same preparation is effective in powder form as an additional measure to

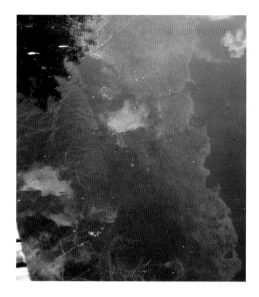

deal with thread algae: 100gm per square metre is spread evenly over the whole water surface. The algae quickly die off and can be scooped off the surface.

Algae Formation

Establishing the causes:

Do ducks visit the pool from time to time?

Is the water cloudy sometimes and do broken off plant parts float round? (rats, mice)

Can surface water get into the pool at any point? (stream, overflow, edge)

Have nearby flowerbeds and grass been fed with artificial fertiliser?

Have blossoms, leaves, or other vegetation entered the water?

Has agricultural land had influence on the water (dust, manure, chaff)?

Have people bathed after using sun lotions and without showering first?

Are large numbers of a variety of underwater plants lacking?

Have adults, children, or dogs walked over the regeneration areas (destruction of vegetation on the shore)?

Are there a lot of frogs in the pool?

Are there fish and/or water turtles in the pool?

Is there a lot of sediment in the pool?

Did any of the water being sucked from the pool re-enter it?

Are there places on the bank where the plants' substrate was washed up (e.g., by rain)?

Has the external gravel filter silted up?

Are phosphate-binding granules being used that have not been replaced for a while?

Is the stream full of debris?

Have 'humus bridges' breached the capillary barrier?

Is the pool often topped up with nutrient-rich water (quality of the water used for filling)?

Does water from any building roofs enter the pool (dust, guano, airborne nutrients, etc.)?

Pool Water Indicators

Clear water: this means there is a biological balance in the water. If in doubt, take a water sample. Every pool owner should be able to measure pH and oxygen levels.

Green clouding: floating algae (green coccus algae) can cloud the water so that you see only a few cm into the water. In spring, and when the pool has just been filled, this can be normal—otherwise it points to too much fertiliser.

Solution: Introduce zoo plankton (Daphne, Cyclops) and perhaps add underwater plants (competition for nutrients).

Brown discolouration: this can be caused by brown floating algae—usually in pools where there is too little light. The green algae that produce oxygen are missing. As is the case with all floating algae, using a microfibre filter can be the answer. It also occurs where there is too much mud, leaves, and decaying plants. If the plants in the pool are well developed, it is not usually a problem; the pool has the character of a 'moorland' lake and is biologically sound. A black liner can often reinforce the impression of a 'moorland' lake.

Yellow discolouration: this occurs because of decaying plant parts—often high concentrations of nitrates —and usually the pH value sinks too. The recommended action is sucking out of sediment and removing decaying matter. If persistent a partial water change should be undertaken.

Milky-cloudy water: this is caused by bacteria, which again can increase massively when too much organic material is present. Usually there are not enough underwater plants that produce oxygen and consume nutrients.

Solution: partial water change, remove organic material, introduce Daphne, aerate.

Foul-smelling water: this is an indication of decay or fermentation—usually blue algae are seen.

Solution: clean pool, change water, aerate.

Source: Richard Weixler

PROBLEM SOLVING

FAULT FINDING CHART

Fault	Possible Cause	Remedy
Circulation pump stopped	Low water level in filter chamber	Check the water levels in the filter chamber. Water may be taking too long to pass through the filter, causing the float switch to operate. Clean the filter or replace the filter cloth as necessary.
	Circuit breaker tripped	Check the control panel main switch and pump circuit breaker. Reset if necessary.
	Control circuit fuse blown	Check fuse F1 in the control panel.
	Time clock settings	Make sure the time clock has not been set to permanently off.
Water not circulating	Water level too low	Check that the mains water top-up is turned on and the water level in the filter chamber is correct. The level should be checked when the pump is switched off.
Water quality deteriorating	Overuse of pool	Increase the number of times the pump runs each day to allow the water to be filtered more frequently.
	Sediment build up in the bottom drain being stirred up by swimmers	Purge the bottom drain by opening the valve until the water runs clear.
Blanket weed and algae in the regeneration zone	Water warming up, particularly in the spring	The algae occur naturally and strong growth may be noticed in the spring before the higher plants have started their growing season. Increase the number of times the pump runs each day so that colder water from the deep swimming area is circulated. Once the plants are more established they will deprive the algae of nutrients.

SEASONAL CHART

SPRING

Water and Plants

Check the water pH with a test kit and adjust if necessary.

Clear any early growth of algae and blanket weed.

Float barley straw up to two months to inhibit algal growth and encourage water fleas. Do not allow to sink.

Carry out any replacement or additional planting.

Divide and transplant marginal and moisture-loving plants where necessary.

Reintroduce any frost-tender plants protected over winter.

Cut back old foliage left over winter to protect plants, taking care not to damage emerging young growth.

Mulch bog gardens and pond and stream margins to reduce weed growth and hold in moisture.

Wildlife

Protect frog spawn and tadpoles and move to another pond if necessary. Remove any fish that may be in the pool.

Structures and Equipment

Clean pond edgings and surrounding surfaces of potentially slippery algae and dirt.

Check pond edgings for looseness or frost damage and carry out any repairs.

Check linings, walls, and copings, waterfalls, and streams for any damage.

Check bridges and decks for rot or corrosion and repair if necessary.

Check electrical equipment and cables for damage.

Service pumps and reinstall where removed over winter.

SUMMER

Water and Plants

Regularly check the water level and top up as necessary.

Check the water pH with a test kit and adjust if necessary.

In very hot, humid weather keep fountains and waterfalls running overnight to maintain oxygen levels.

Remove algae and blanket weed regularly if necessary.

Regularly remove dead and dying leaves on all pond plants.

Regularly deadhead flowering plants, particularly water lilies.

Check plants for signs of pests or disease and treat if necessary.

Divide and transplant established water lilies.

Wildlife

Add protective nets or wires to deter pond predators (herons and pets) where necessary.

Check whether there is enough zoological plankton in the water. Simply hold a white porcelain plate at a depth of 50cm and observe what moves over it.

Structures and Equipment

Clean biological filters to ensure the free flow of water.

Regularly clean fountain and waterfall pump strainers and filters to ensure efficient operation.

AUTUMN

Water and Plants

Remove dead and dying leaves from marginal plants and water lilies.

Cut back and remove excessive growth on submerged plants before natural dieback and subsequent decay occur.

Protect tender bog or moisture-loving plants with a thick mulch or by folding their decaying leaves onto the plant's crown.

Leave reeds alone.

Wildlife

Cut back plants.

Provide a rock or log piles close to the pond for newts to hibernate under.

Leave some pond-side vegetation in place as cover for frogs and toads.

Allow some stems of marginal plants to remain standing.

Leave some dead seed heads on plants for over-wintering invertebrates.

Structures and Equipment

Place nets in position to catch autumn leaf fall and remove the leaves regularly.

Remove netting before the first snowfall.

Remove, clean, and store pumps, filters, and lights where not required over winter.

WINTER

Water and Plants

Keep an area of water free from ice during extreme weather to avoid a build-up of toxic gases.

Brush snow from ice-covered ponds to allow light penetration and speed the melting of the ice.

Clear any remaining dead vegetation from the water before it decays.

Apply a mulch of compost or well-rotted manure to pond-side plants.

Wildlife

Disrupt the pond as little as possible to avoid disturbing hibernating pond life.

Establish whether creatures are crawling around on the bottom of the pool that have over-wintered there and are trying to reach the shallower areas to lay eggs. Remove them with a fishing net, as they could die otherwise.

Structures and Equipment

Install a water heater to keep an area of ice-free water.

Float a flexible rubber ball on the water to absorb the pressure of expanding ice and remove daily to keep an ice-free area.

Remove the net before first snowfall.

10

CONSTRUCTION DETAILS

EXCAVATION

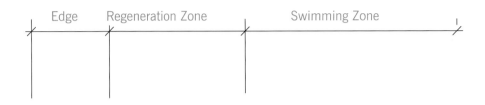

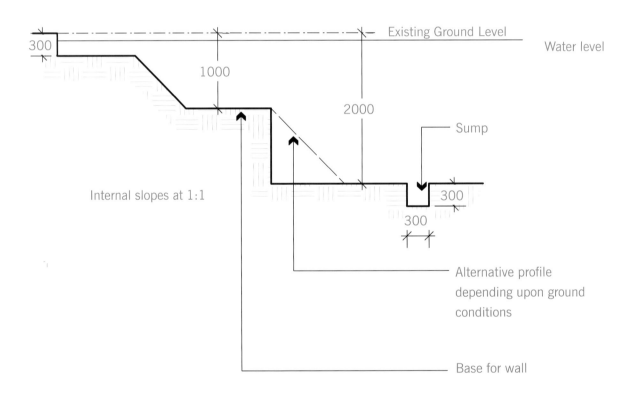

SECTION   Scale: NTS

Excavation for Half-Depth Walls

LINER JOINTING

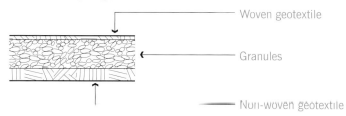

Woven geotextile

Granules

Non-woven geotextile

BENTOMITE MATTING

JOINING BENTOMAT
Overlap layers of
Bentomat and spread
granules of bentomite
between the layers and
press layers firmly
together. Granules will
swell when wet, providing
a watertight seal.

JOINING LAYERS

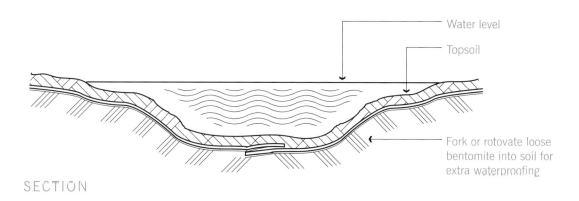

Water level

Topsoil

Fork or rotovate loose
bentomite into soil for
extra waterproofing

SECTION

LAYING BENTOMAT
Spread the bentomat
over the surface of the
pond and up the sides.
Firm down and cover
with a layer of topsoil

LAYING PROCEDURE

Liner Jointing

WALLS

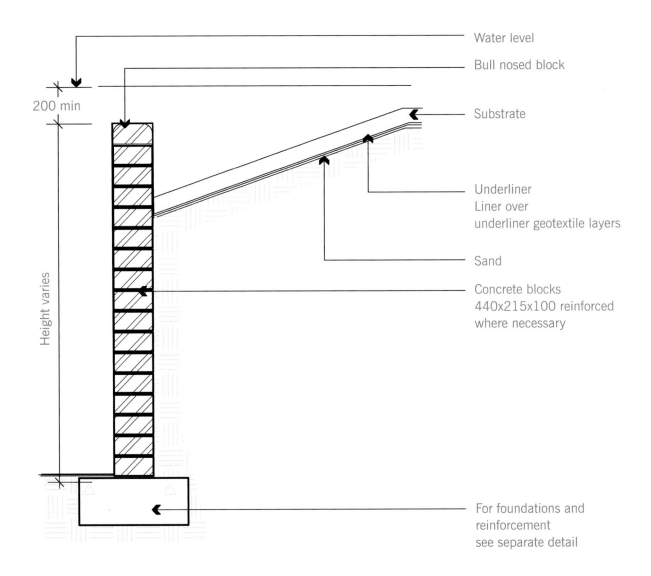

Water level

Bull nosed block

200 min

Substrate

Height varies

Underliner
Liner over
underliner geotextile layers

Sand

Concrete blocks
440x215x100 reinforced
where necessary

For foundations and
reinforcement
see separate detail

Note: All walls with height greater
than 900mm should be
referred to a structural
engineer for final approval

Wall – Full Depth Concrete block

Scale 1:20

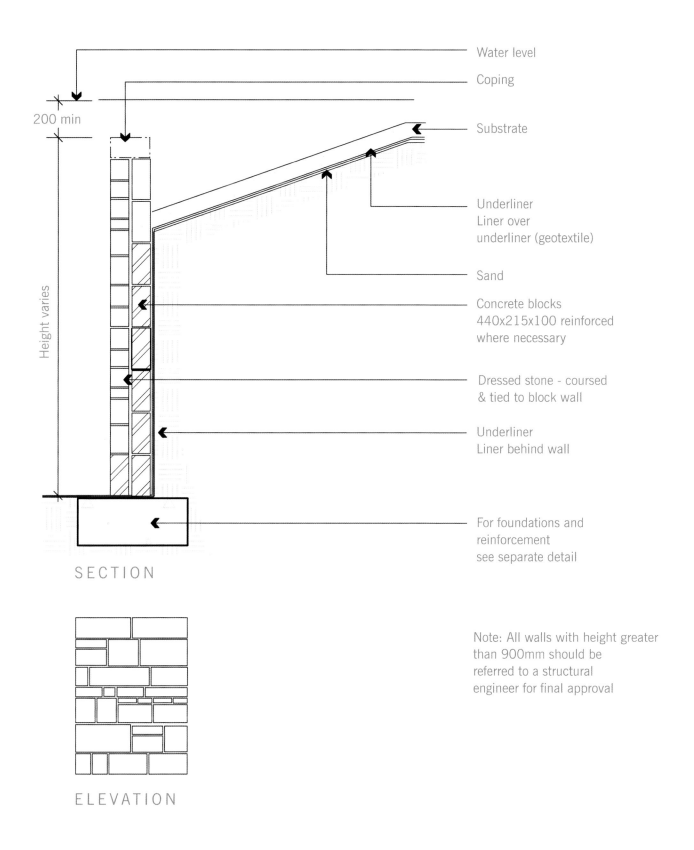

Water level

Coping

200 min

Substrate

Underliner
Liner over
underliner (geotextile)

Sand

Concrete blocks
440x215x100 reinforced
where necessary

Height varies

Dressed stone - coursed
& tied to block wall

Underliner
Liner behind wall

For foundations and
reinforcement
see separate detail

SECTION

ELEVATION

Note: All walls with height greater
than 900mm should be
referred to a structural
engineer for final approval

Wall – Full Depth stone faced

Scale 1:20

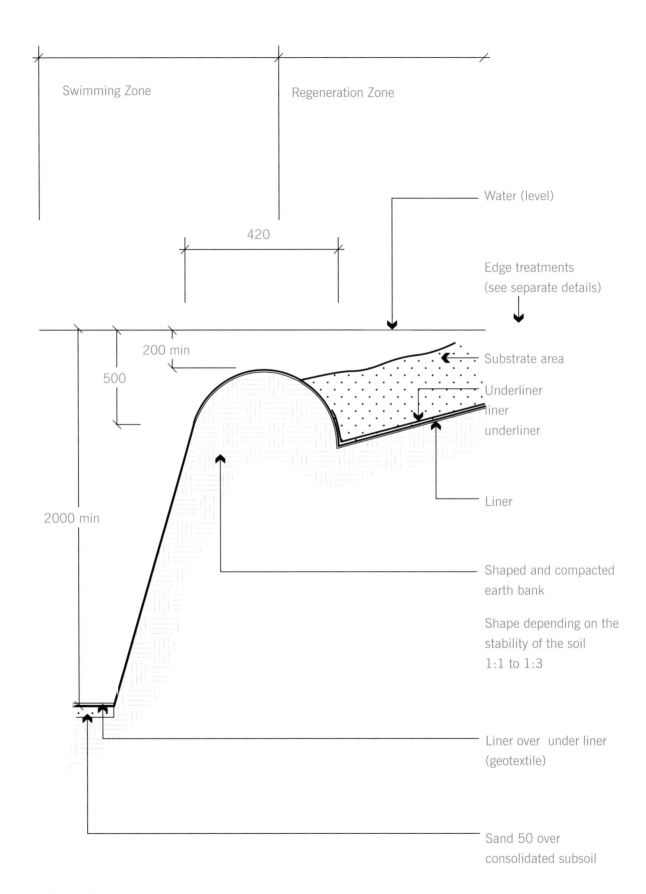

Swimming Zone

Regeneration Zone

420

Water (level)

Edge treatments
(see separate details)

200 min

500

Substrate area

Underliner

liner

underliner

Liner

2000 min

Shaped and compacted
earth bank

Shape depending on the
stability of the soil
1:1 to 1:3

Liner over under liner
(geotextile)

Sand 50 over
consolidated subsoil

Wall – Full Depth Earth bank method

Scale 1:20

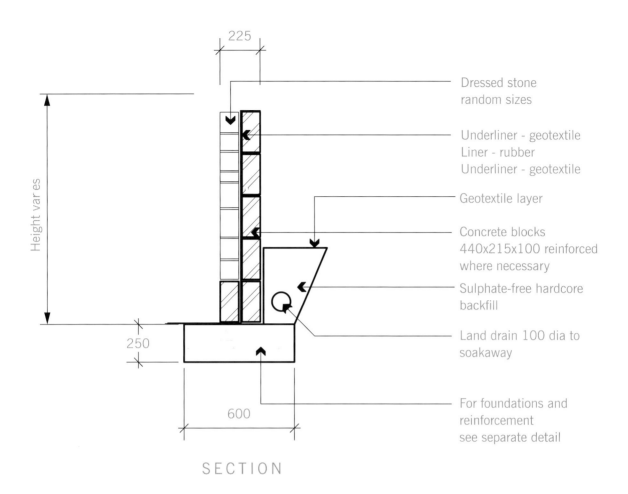

225

Dressed stone
random sizes

Underliner - geotextile
Liner - rubber
Underliner - geotextile

Geotextile layer

Concrete blocks
440x215x100 reinforced
where necessary

Sulphate-free hardcore
backfill

Land drain 100 dia to
soakaway

For foundations and
reinforcement
see separate detail

Height varies

250

600

SECTION

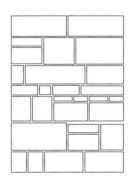

ELEVATION

Wall – Half-Depth Stone faced

Scale 1:20

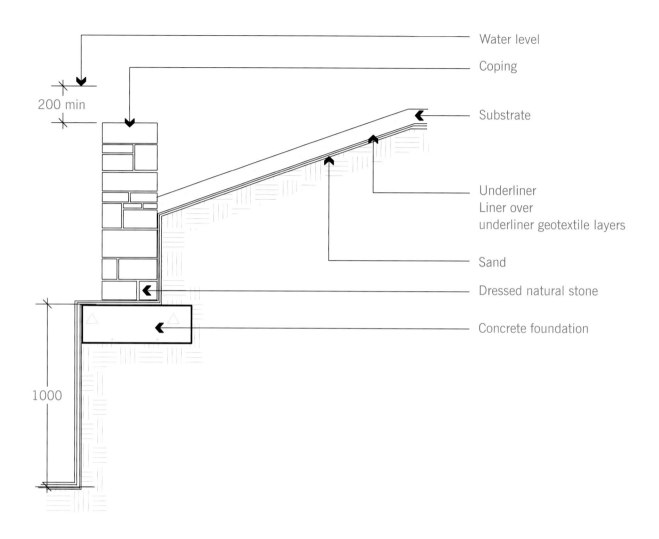

Water level

Coping

Substrate

200 min

Underliner
Liner over
underliner geotextile layers

Sand

Dressed natural stone

Concrete foundation

1000

Wall – Half-Depth Stone natural coursed

Scale 1:20

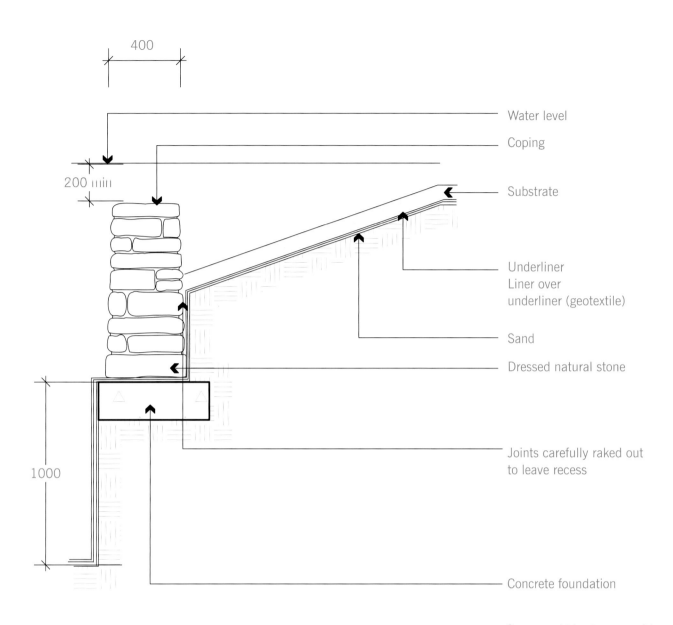

400

200 min

1000

Water level

Coping

Substrate

Underliner
Liner over
underliner (geotextile)

Sand

Dressed natural stone

Joints carefully raked out
to leave recess

Concrete foundation

Square rubble stone roughly
coursed. Vary size of stone
- lay two small over one large
Use plenty of mortar to
bed the stones

Wall – Half-Depth Stone natural uncoursed

Scale 1:20

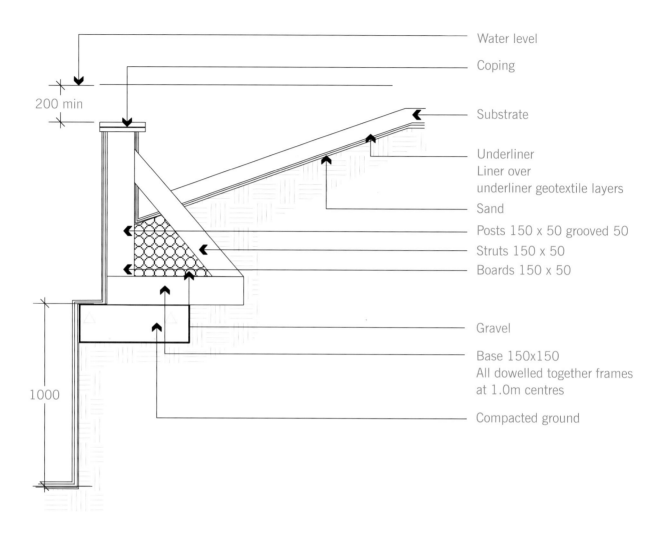

Water level

Coping

200 min

Substrate

Underliner
Liner over
underliner geotextile layers

Sand

Posts 150 x 50 grooved 50

Struts 150 x 50

Boards 150 x 50

Gravel

Base 150x150
All dowelled together frames
at 1.0m centres

1000

Compacted ground

Wall – Half-Depth Timber

Scale 1:20

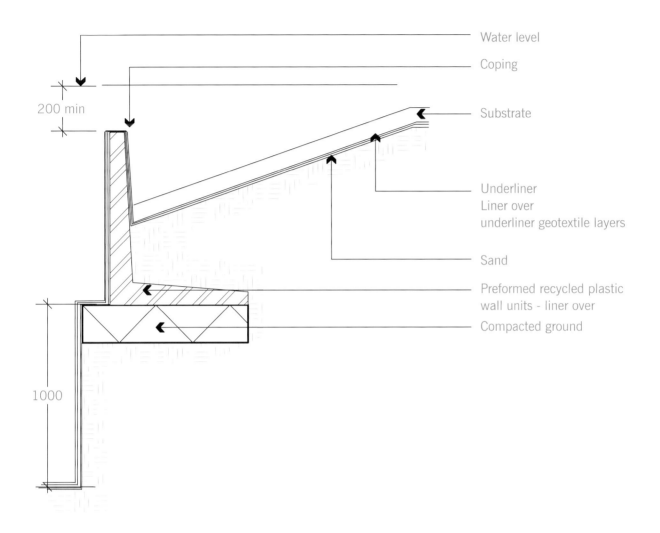

Water level

Coping

200 min

Substrate

Underliner
Liner over
underliner geotextile layers

Sand

Preformed recycled plastic
wall units - liner over

Compacted ground

1000

Wall – Half-Depth Recycled plastic units   Scale 1:20

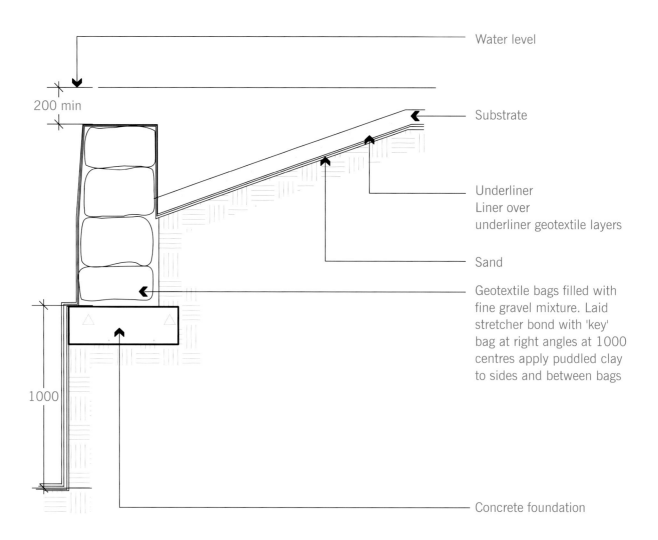

Water level

200 min

Substrate

Underliner
Liner over
underliner geotextile layers

Sand

Geotextile bags filled with
fine gravel mixture. Laid
stretcher bond with 'key'
bag at right angles at 1000
centres apply puddled clay
to sides and between bags

1000

Concrete foundation

Wall – Half-Depth Geotextile bags/sacks

Scale 1:20

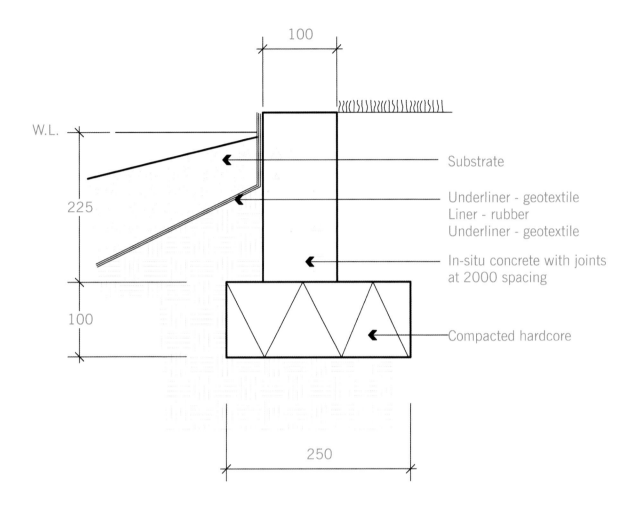

100

W.L.

225

100

250

Substrate

Underliner - geotextile
Liner - rubber
Underliner - geotextile

In-situ concrete with joints
at 2000 spacing

Compacted hardcore

Perimeter Wall Concrete block

Scale 1:5

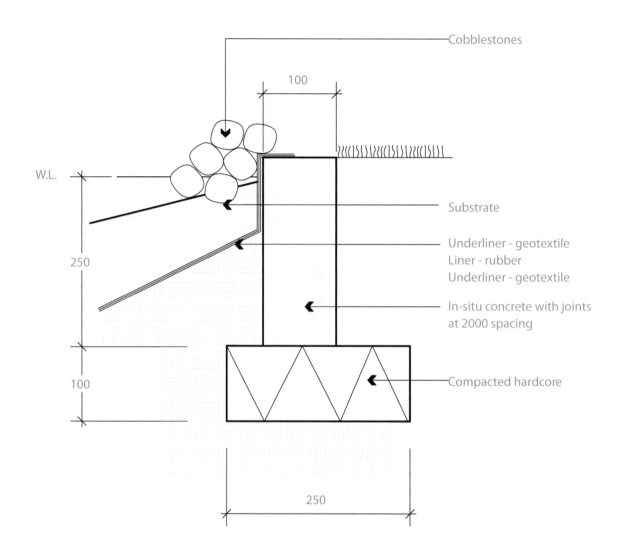

Cobblestones

100

Substrate

Underliner - geotextile
Liner - rubber
Underliner - geotextile

In-situ concrete with joints
at 2000 spacing

Compacted hardcore

W.L.

250

100

250

Perimeter Wall Concrete in-situ

Scale 1:5

EDGES & BEACHES

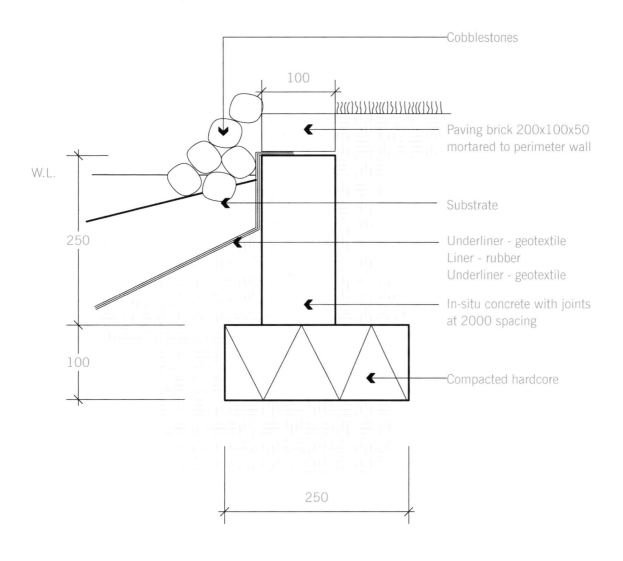

Cobblestones

100

Paving brick 200x100x50
mortared to perimeter wall

W.L.

250

Substrate

Underliner - geotextile
Liner - rubber
Underliner - geotextile

In-situ concrete with joints
at 2000 spacing

100

Compacted hardcore

250

Edge Paving/brick

Scale 1:5

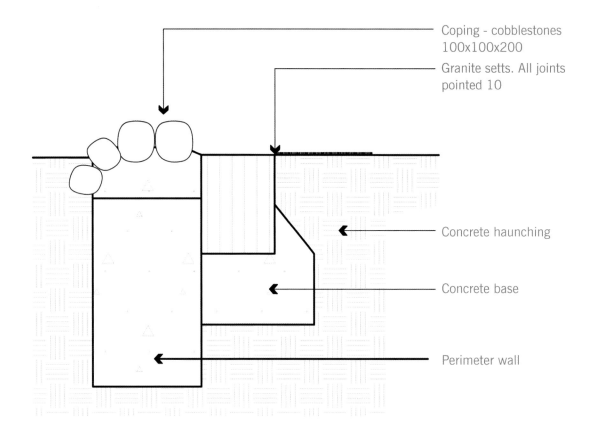

Coping - cobblestones
100x100x200

Granite setts. All joints
pointed 10

Concrete haunching

Concrete base

Perimeter wall

Edge Granite sett

Scale 1:5

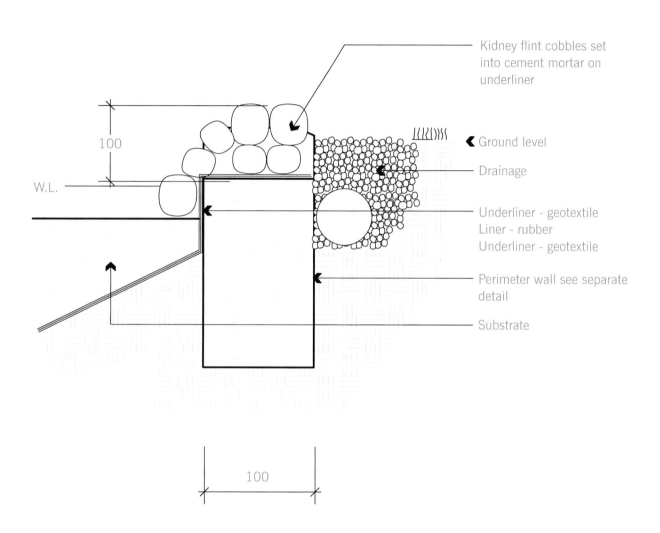

Kidney flint cobbles set
into cement mortar on
underliner

❮ Ground level

Drainage

Underliner - geotextile
Liner - rubber
Underliner - geotextile

Perimeter wall see separate
detail

Substrate

100

W.L.

100

Edge Cobblestones

Scale 1:5

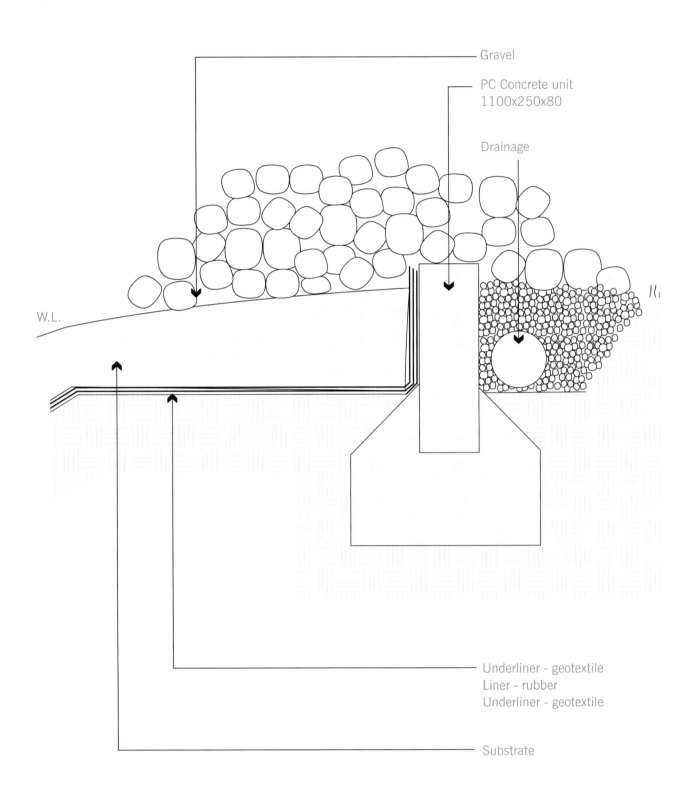

Gravel

PC Concrete unit
1100x250x80

Drainage

W.L.

Underliner - geotextile
Liner - rubber
Underliner - geotextile

Substrate

Edge Pre-cast concrete unit

Scale 1:5

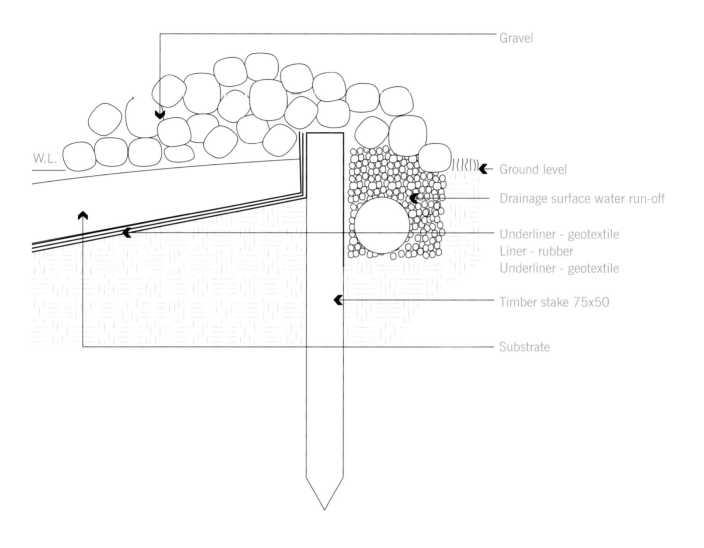

Gravel

W.L.

Ground level

Drainage surface water run-off

Underliner - geotextile
Liner - rubber
Underliner - geotextile

Timber stake 75x50

Substrate

Edge Timber

Scale 1:5

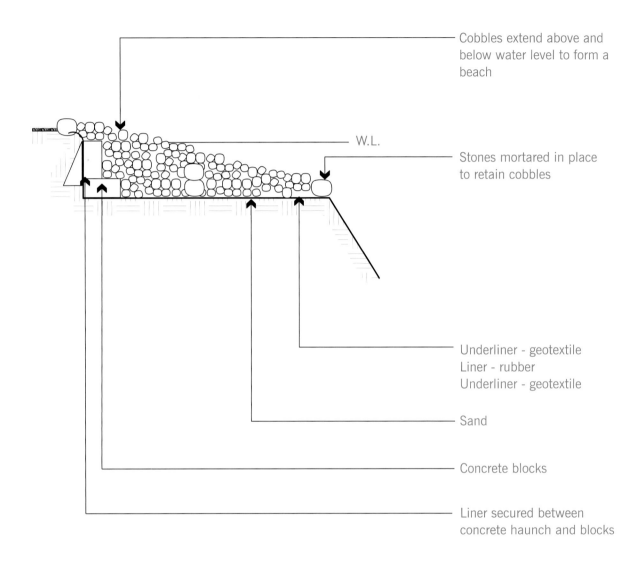

Cobbles extend above and below water level to form a beach

W.L.

Stones mortared in place to retain cobbles

Underliner - geotextile
Liner - rubber
Underliner - geotextile

Sand

Concrete blocks

Liner secured between concrete haunch and blocks

Beach Cobblestones

Scale 1:20

STEPS & LADDERS

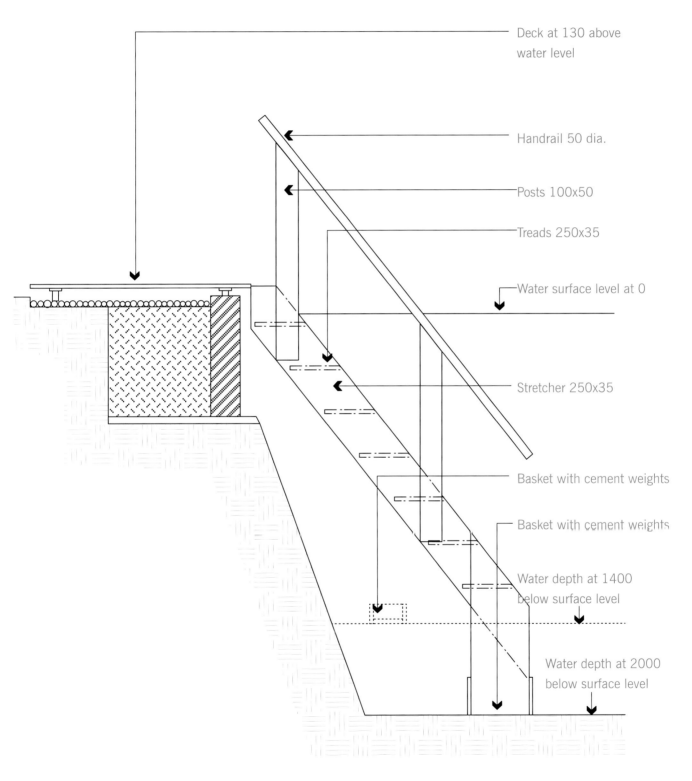

Deck at 130 above water level

Handrail 50 dia.

Posts 100x50

Treads 250x35

Water surface level at 0

Stretcher 250x35

Basket with cement weights

Basket with cement weights

Water depth at 1400 below surface level

Water depth at 2000 below surface level

Steps Timber

Scale 1:20

197

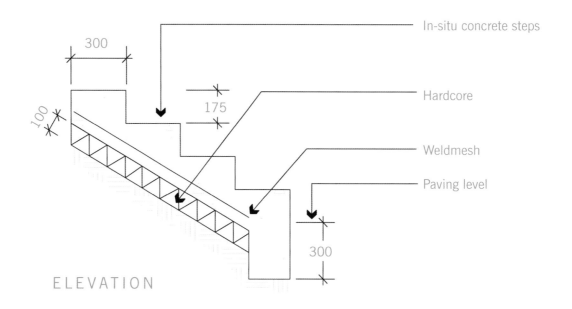

300

100

175

In-situ concrete steps

Hardcore

Weldmesh

Paving level

300

ELEVATION

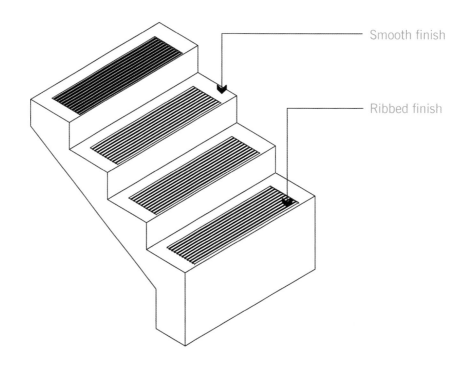

Smooth finish

Ribbed finish

ISOMETRIC VIEW

Steps Concrete in-situ

Scale 1:20

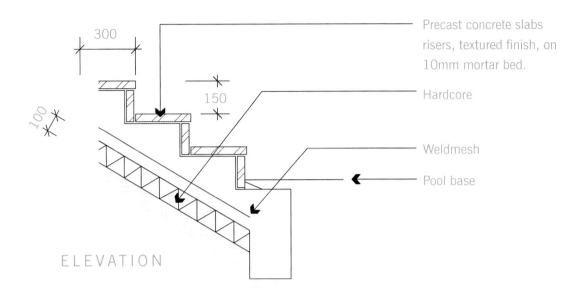

300

150

100

Precast concrete slabs
risers, textured finish, on
10mm mortar bed.

Hardcore

Weldmesh

Pool base

ELEVATION

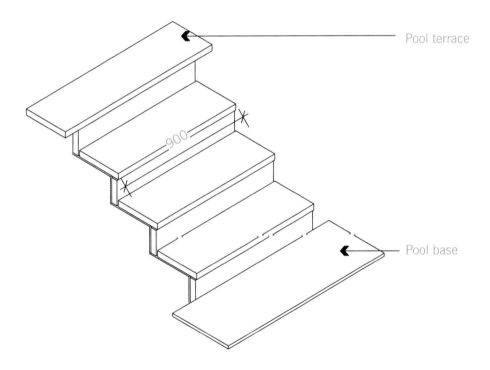

Pool terrace

900

Pool base

ISOMETRIC VIEW

Steps Concrete slab

Scale 1:20

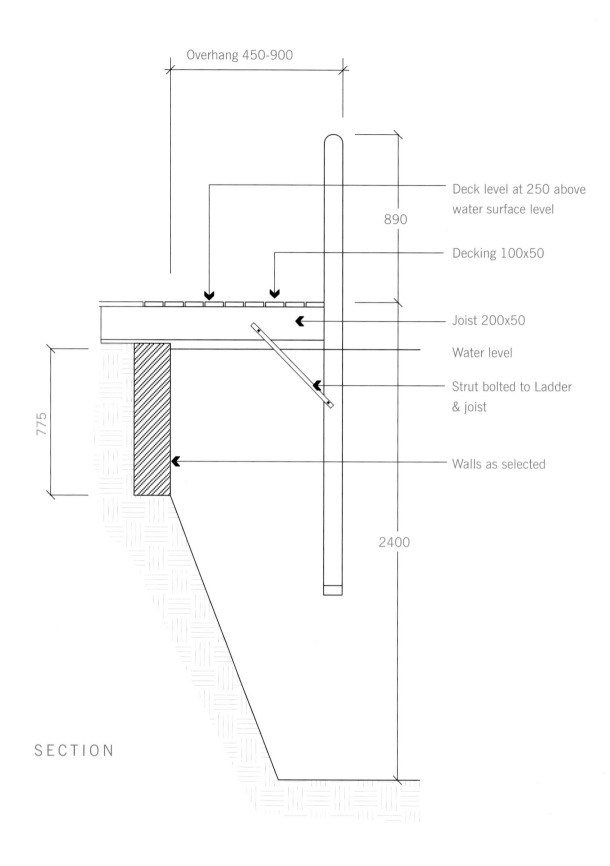

Overhang 450-900

Deck level at 250 above
water surface level

Decking 100x50

890

Joist 200x50

Water level

Strut bolted to Ladder
& joist

775

Walls as selected

2400

SECTION

Ladder Timber

Scale 1:20

200

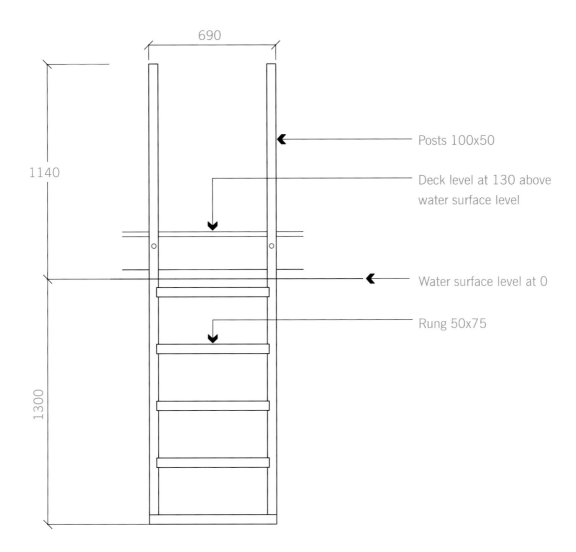

690

1140

1300

Posts 100x50

Deck level at 130 above
water surface level

Water surface level at 0

Rung 50x75

ELEVATION

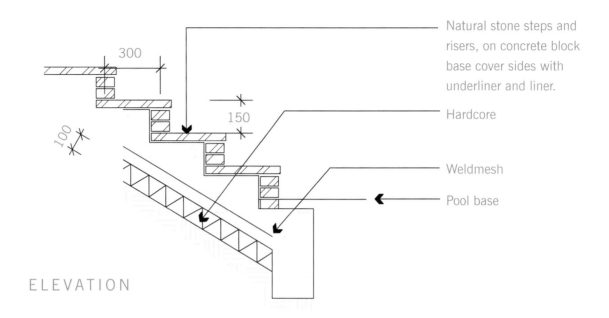

300

150

100

Natural stone steps and risers, on concrete block base cover sides with underliner and liner.

Hardcore

Weldmesh

Pool base

ELEVATION

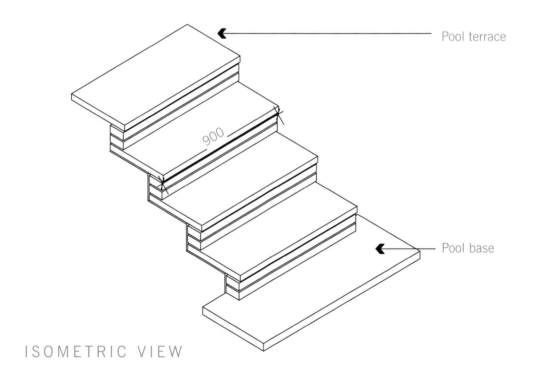

Pool terrace

900

Pool base

ISOMETRIC VIEW

Steps Natural stone

Scale 1:20

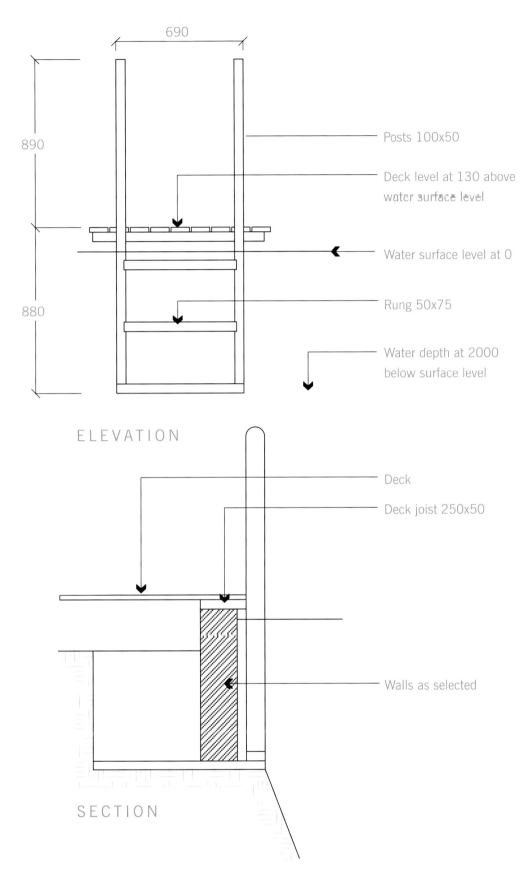

690

890

880

Posts 100x50

Deck level at 130 above
water surface level

Water surface level at 0

Rung 50x75

Water depth at 2000
below surface level

ELEVATION

Deck

Deck joist 250x50

Walls as selected

SECTION

Ladder Timber

Scale 1:20

STREAMS & WATERFALLS

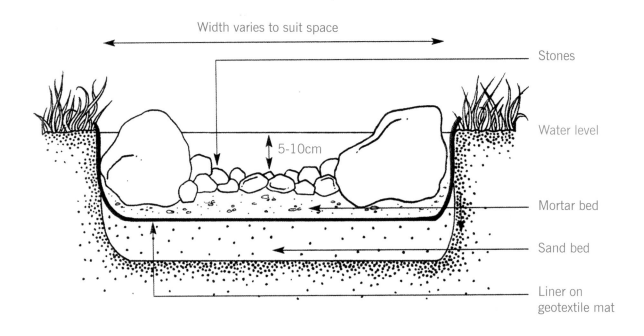

Width varies to suit space

Stones

Water level

5-10cm

Mortar bed

Sand bed

Liner on geotextile mat

Stream

Scale 1:20

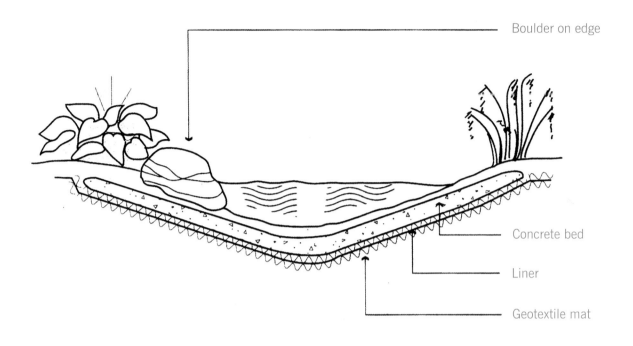

Boulder on edge

Concrete bed

Liner

Geotextile mat

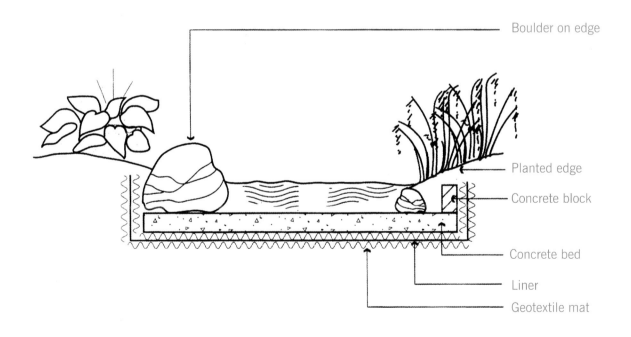

Boulder on edge

Planted edge

Concrete block

Concrete bed

Liner

Geotextile mat

Stream Profiles

Scale 1:20

205

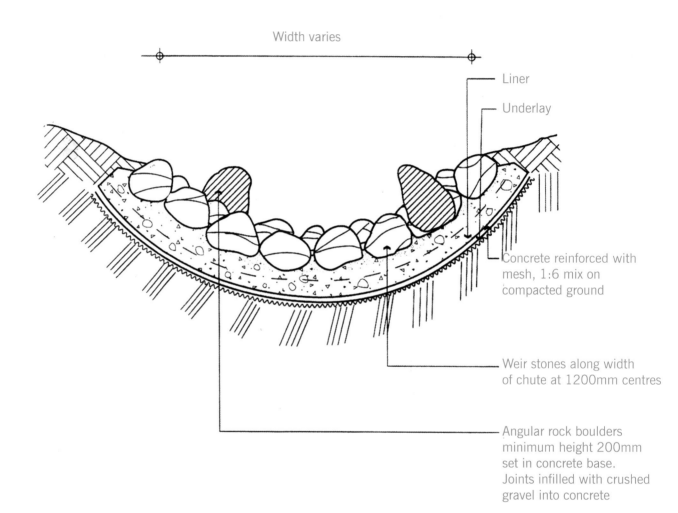

Width varies

Liner

Underlay

Concrete reinforced with mesh, 1:6 mix on compacted ground

Weir stones along width of chute at 1200mm centres

Angular rock boulders minimum height 200mm set in concrete base. Joints infilled with crushed gravel into concrete

Stream Stone bed channel

Scale 1:10

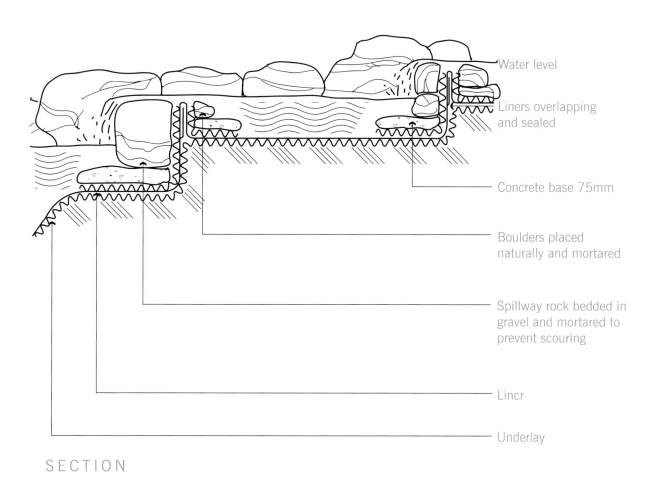

Water level

Liners overlapping
and sealed

Concrete base 75mm

Boulders placed
naturally and mortared

Spillway rock bedded in
gravel and mortared to
prevent scouring

Lincr

Underlay

S E C T I O N

Waterfall

Scale 1:20

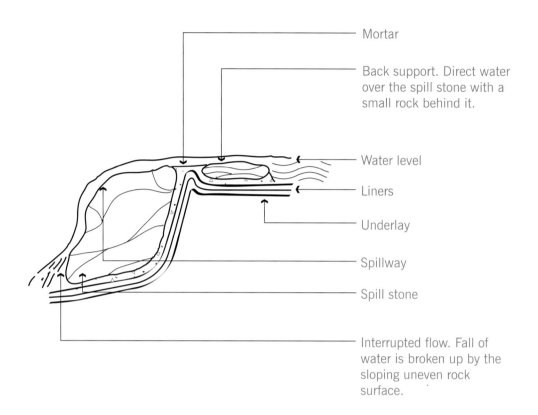

Mortar

Back support. Direct water over the spill stone with a small rock behind it.

Water level

Liners

Underlay

Spillway

Spill stone

Interrupted flow. Fall of water is broken up by the sloping uneven rock surface.

SECTION

Waterfall Interrupted flow

Scale 1:20

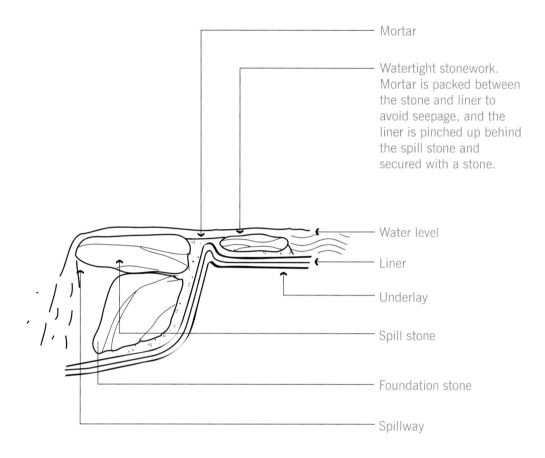

Mortar

Watertight stonework.
Mortar is packed between
the stone and liner to
avoid seepage, and the
liner is pinched up behind
the spill stone and
secured with a stone.

Water level

Liner

Underlay

Spill stone

Foundation stone

Spillway

SECTION

Waterfall Unbroken flow

Scale 1:20

DECKS & BOARDWALKS

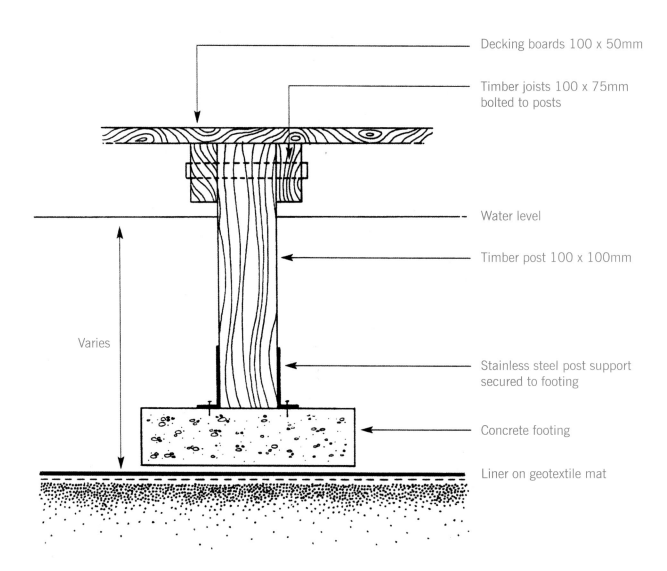

Decking boards 100 x 50mm

Timber joists 100 x 75mm
bolted to posts

Water level

Timber post 100 x 100mm

Varies

Stainless steel post support
secured to footing

Concrete footing

Liner on geotextile mat

Decking Timber support   Scale NTS

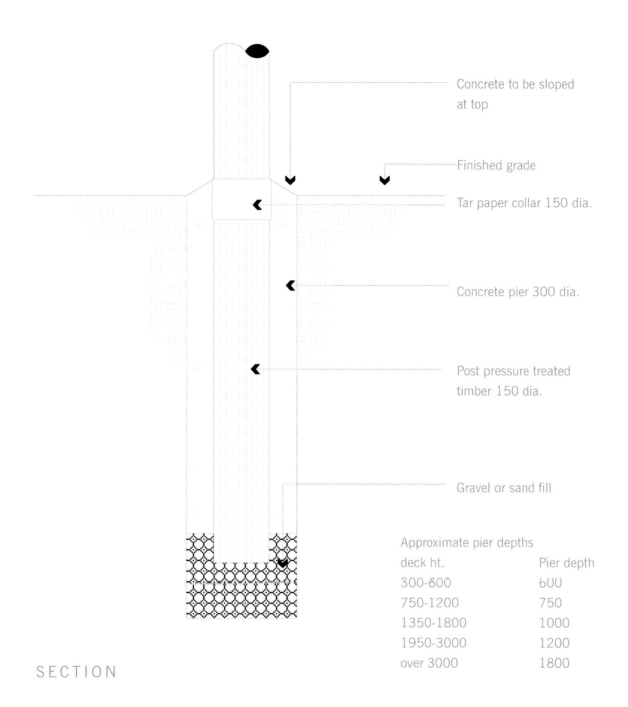

Concrete to be sloped
at top

Finished grade

Tar paper collar 150 dia.

Concrete pier 300 dia.

Post pressure treated
timber 150 dia.

Gravel or sand fill

Approximate pier depths

deck ht.	Pier depth
300-600	600
750-1200	750
1350-1800	1000
1950-3000	1200
over 3000	1800

SECTION

Timber Deck Post support (typical)

Scale 1:10

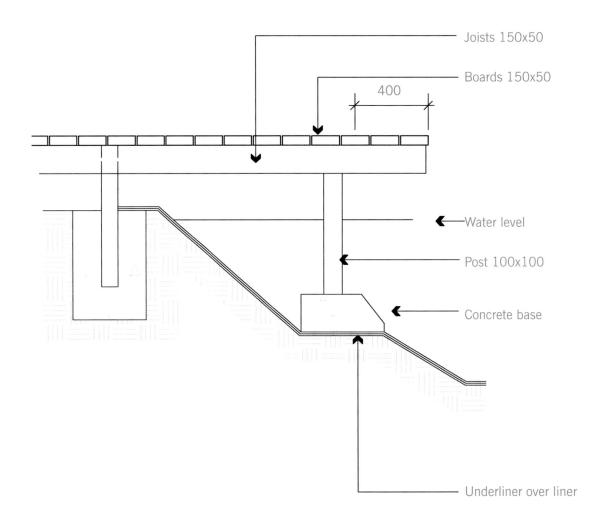

Joists 150x50

Boards 150x50

400

Water level

Post 100x100

Concrete base

Underliner over liner

SECTION

Timber Deck Over water

Scale 1:20

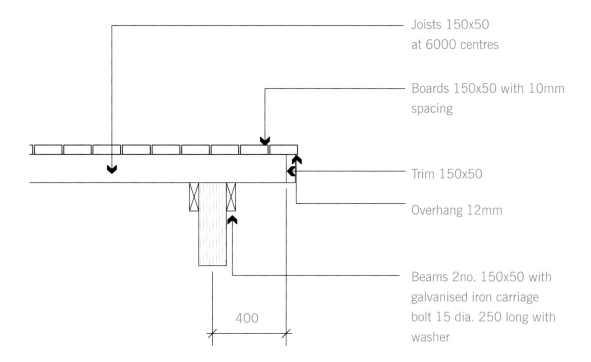

Joists 150x50
at 6000 centres

Boards 150x50 with 10mm
spacing

Trim 150x50

Overhang 12mm

Beams 2no. 150x50 with
galvanised iron carriage
bolt 15 dia. 250 long with
washer

400

SECTION

Timber Deck Edge (with trim)

Scale 1:10

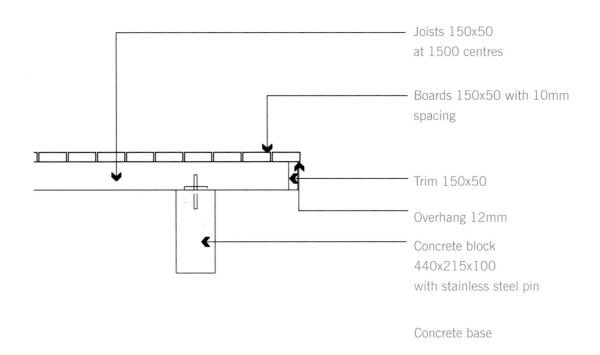

Joists 150x50
at 1500 centres

Boards 150x50 with 10mm
spacing

Trim 150x50

Overhang 12mm

Concrete block
440x215x100
with stainless steel pin

Concrete base

SECTION

Timber Deck Steel pin

Scale 1:20

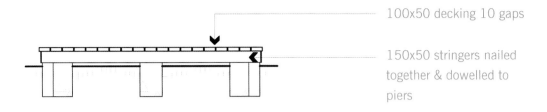

100x50 decking 10 gaps

150x50 stringers nailed
together & dowelled to
piers

S E C T I O N

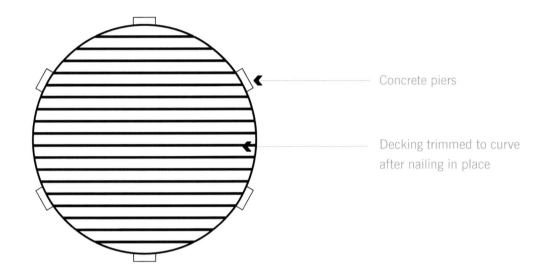

Concrete piers

Decking trimmed to curve
after nailing in place

P L A N

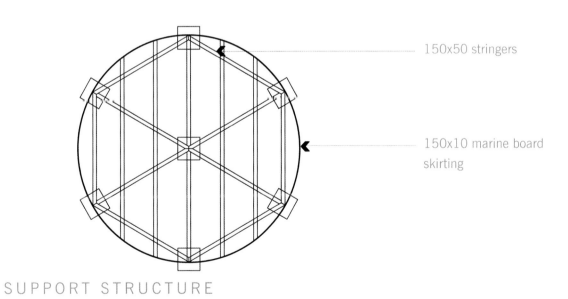

150x50 stringers

150x10 marine board
skirting

S U P P O R T   S T R U C T U R E

Timber Deck Circular

Scale 1:50

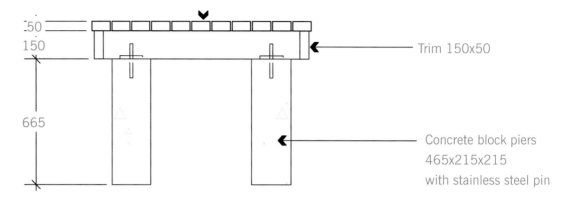

Boards 100x50 with 10mm
spacing

Joists 150x50
at 1500 centres

50
150

665

Trim 150x50

Concrete block piers
465x215x215
with stainless steel pin

ELEVATION

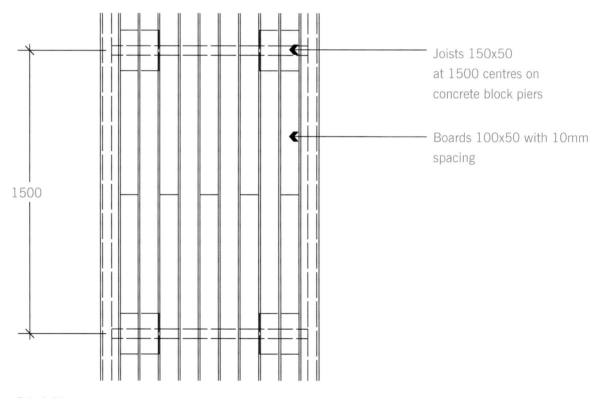

Joists 150x50
at 1500 centres on
concrete block piers

Boards 100x50 with 10mm
spacing

1500

PLAN

Boardwalk Timber

Scale 1:20

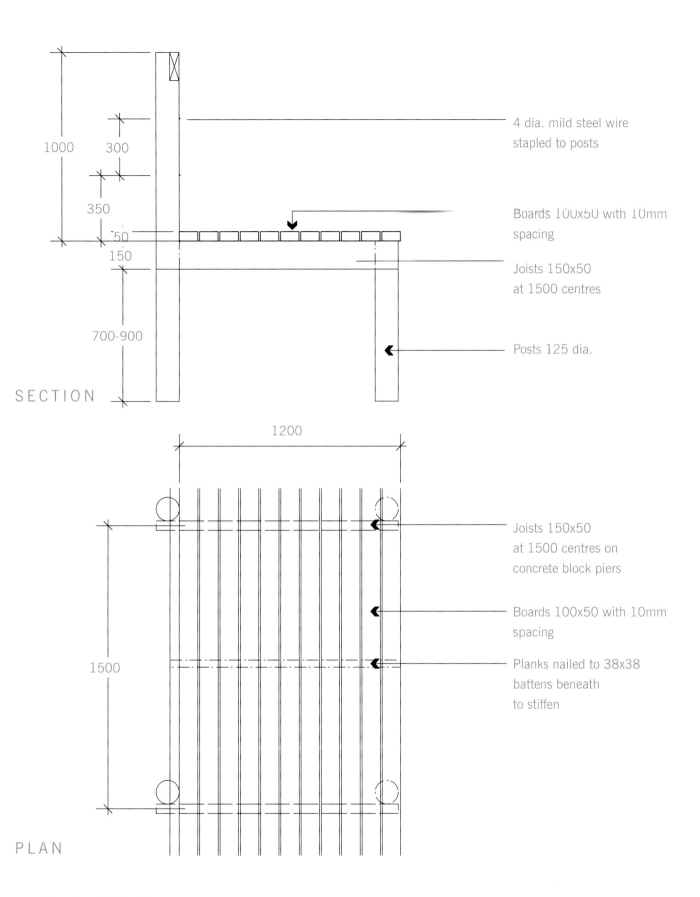

1000

300

350

50

150

700-900

SECTION

4 dia. mild steel wire
stapled to posts

Boards 100x50 with 10mm
spacing

Joists 150x50
at 1500 centres

Posts 125 dia.

1200

1500

PLAN

Joists 150x50
at 1500 centres on
concrete block piers

Boards 100x50 with 10mm
spacing

Planks nailed to 38x38
battens beneath
to stiffen

Boardwalk Timber

Scale 1:20

BRIDGES & JETTIES

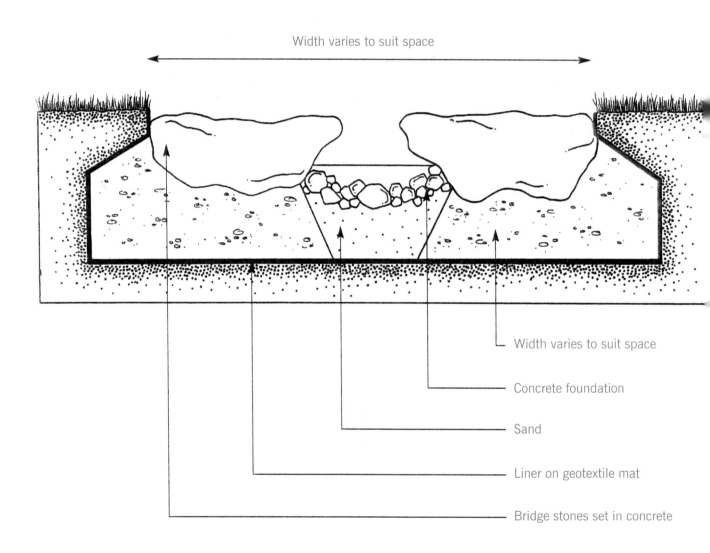

Width varies to suit space

Width varies to suit space

Concrete foundation

Sand

Liner on geotextile mat

Bridge stones set in concrete

Bridge Stone

Scale 1:20

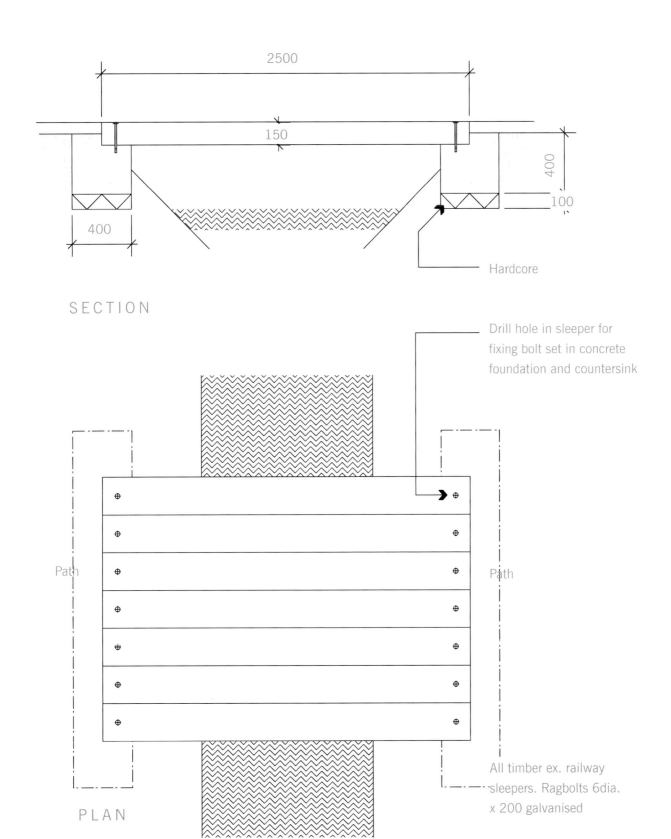

2500

150

400

100

400

SECTION

Hardcore

Drill hole in sleeper for
fixing bolt set in concrete
foundation and countersink

Path

Path

PLAN

Stream

All timber ex. railway
sleepers. Ragbolts 6dia.
x 200 galvanised

Footbridge Timber (small)

Scale 1:25

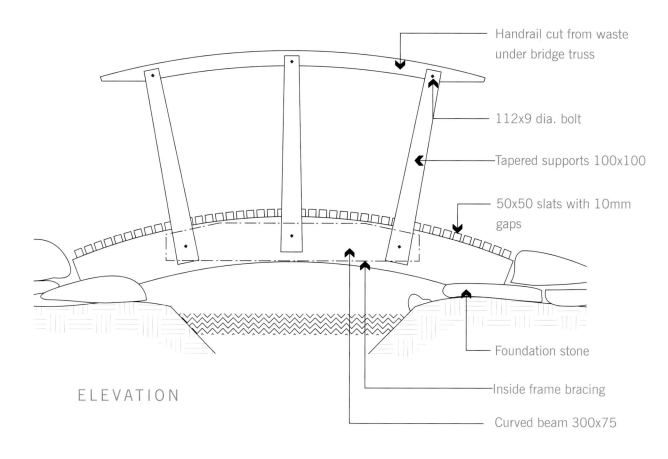

Handrail cut from waste under bridge truss

112x9 dia. bolt

Tapered supports 100x100

50x50 slats with 10mm gaps

Foundation stone

Inside frame bracing

Curved beam 300x75

ELEVATION

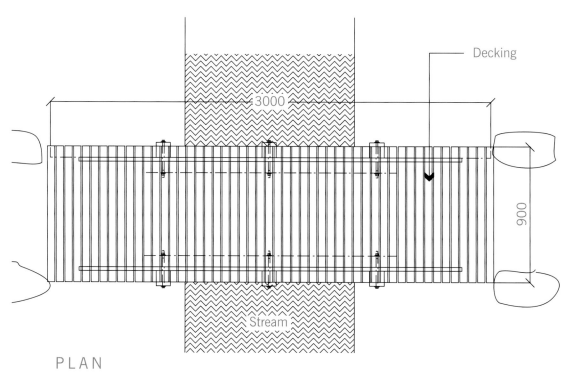

Decking

3000

900

Stream

PLAN

Footbridge Timber

Scale 1:25

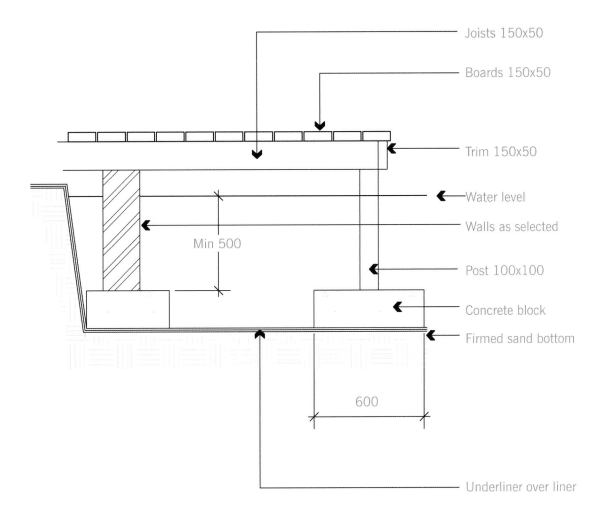

Joists 150x50

Boards 150x50

Trim 150x50

Water level

Walls as selected

Min 500

Post 100x100

Concrete block

Firmed sand bottom

600

Underliner over liner

SECTION

Jetty Timber

Scale 1:20

LIGHTING

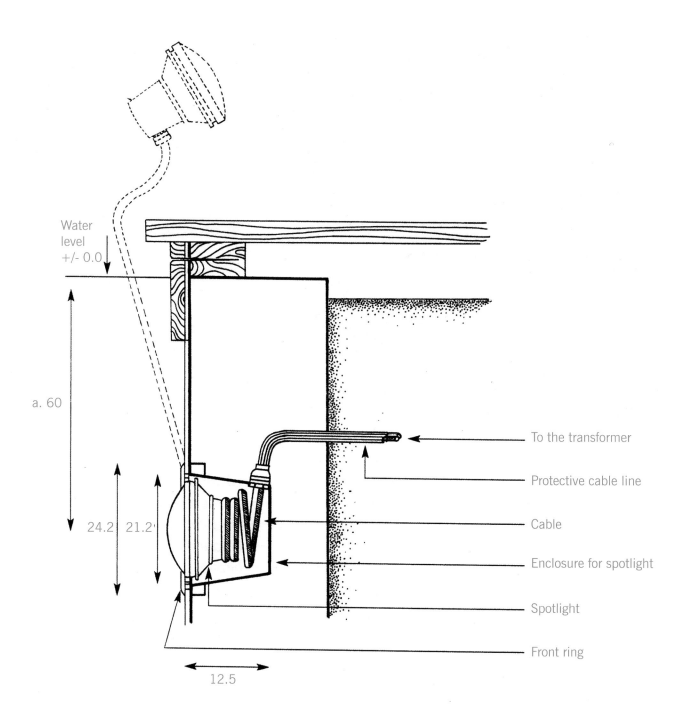

Water level +/- 0.0

a. 60

24.2 | 21.2

12.5

To the transformer

Protective cable line

Cable

Enclosure for spotlight

Spotlight

Front ring

Lighting Underwater

Scale 1:10

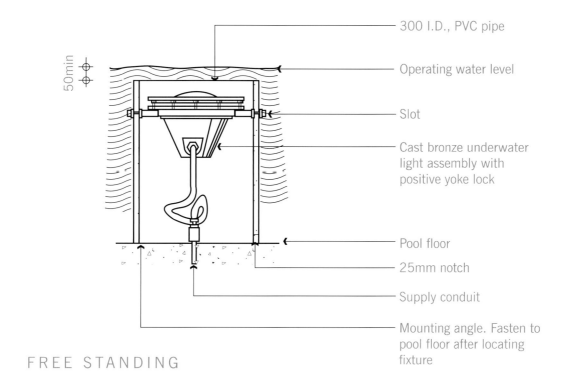

300 I.D., PVC pipe

Operating water level

Slot

Cast bronze underwater light assembly with positive yoke lock

Pool floor

25mm notch

Supply conduit

Mounting angle. Fasten to pool floor after locating fixture

50min

FREE STANDING

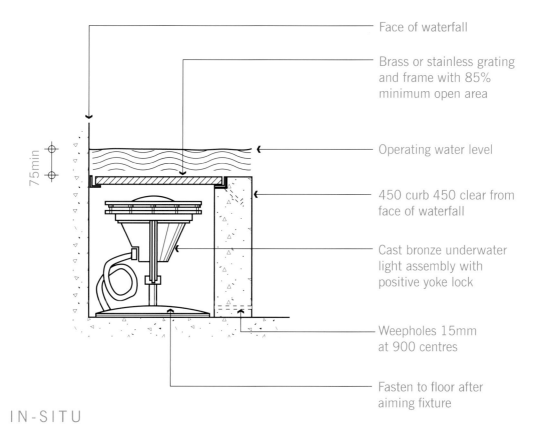

Face of waterfall

Brass or stainless grating and frame with 85% minimum open area

Operating water level

450 curb 450 clear from face of waterfall

Cast bronze underwater light assembly with positive yoke lock

Weepholes 15mm at 900 centres

Fasten to floor after aiming fixture

75min

IN-SITU

Pool Lighting Contained

Scale 1:10

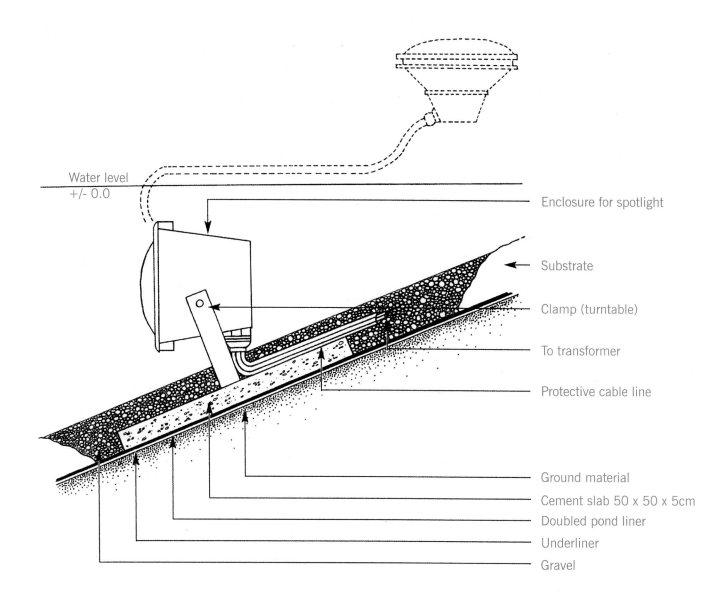

Water level
+/- 0.0

Enclosure for spotlight

Substrate

Clamp (turntable)

To transformer

Protective cable line

Ground material

Cement slab 50 x 50 x 5cm

Doubled pond liner

Underliner

Gravel

Lighting Underwater

Scale 1:10

Photo: Stefan Lehnert – Bioteich

Photo: Stefan Lehnert – Bioteich

11

INFORMATION

HEALTH & SAFETY

Alongside all the benefits of having a natural swimming pool, it must always be remembered that water is potentially dangerous, especially for children. It is vital that you incorporate safety considerations into your design so that you can then enjoy your pool not having to worry about the possibility of an accident. The legal aspects of health and safety are discussed on page 53. This appendix covers the additional aspects of ensuring the health and safety of a natural pool.

Safety During the Building Process

If you have young children, or if children visit your garden—whether by invitation or otherwise—you need to ensure they cannot access the building area unsupervised during

the construction process. A separate fence around the building site is not necessary provided that your property boundaries are secure. If, however, children can gain access to your garden, or if you have children of your own, it may be necessary to erect a temporary security fence around the building area. Machinery, equipment, and materials should be kept in a secure, enclosed area.

If you are involved in the building of your pool, you also need to consider your personal safety during construction. Wear thick gloves to protect your hands, and wear goggles when using tools like drills, chisels, grinders, or sledge hammers. A hard hat and safety footwear are advisable when any heavy building work is in progress. Use additional protective clothing as necessary when using power tools. Ensure that you lift heavy weights safely, calling in help wherever necessary, and that you are fully competent to operate any machinery.

Security Fences

Unless your garden is completely secure and never used by children, the pool area needs to be completely enclosed by a high fence or dense hedge to prevent accidents. In some countries, including the United States, Australia and New Zealand, a fence around a swimming pool is mandatory.

A fence need not detract from the aesthetic appeal of your pool, and can be incorporated into the design. By enclosing your pool, you create a space set apart from the outside world. A fence or hedge can create an attractive backdrop to the pool and provide sanctuary, privacy and sound insulation as well as safety and security. You can satisfy safety criteria and enhance your pool at the same time.

A fence needs to be constructed from sturdy wire mesh or wooden slats, but it can then be clothed in shrubs or climbers, so that in

time it becomes invisible. Alternatively, you could plant a hedge around the pool—but you would then also need to erect a temporary fence to ensure safety until the hedge has become tall and dense enough to prevent access. The design of a fence needs to be such that there are no footholds that would enable a determined child to climb over it. It is important, however, to ensure that wildlife still has access to the pool. To achieve this, leave a gap of about 12cm between the ground and the bottom of the fence. The fence should meet the following criteria, unless your local building regulations specify otherwise:

Minimum height: 1m
Distance between horizontal slats ≤ 4cm
Distance between vertical slats ≤ 11cm
Ground clearance ≤ 12cm
Door/gate with childproof lock

Safety for children

Young children should never play unsupervised in a garden in which there is a body of water. Even shallow water can be fatal. You can teach your own children about the need to respect water, but it is harder to deal with other children, who will be attracted to the pool, possibly in your absence. Make sure that visiting children are quickly acquainted with the dangers and with the rules for use of the pool, and that they are always supervised.

Shallow play areas are a good place to let children gain their first experience of water. They should be taught that they may only enter the pool with floats until they can swim confidently. If the pool ices over in winter, there is the additional danger of children venturing on the ice and falling through it. Make sure they know that they must never walk on ice unless an adult has checked that it is safe, and that they may only do so when an adult is present.

Surfaces and Structures

All swimming pools that are used by children or the elderly should be built with a shallow end and a safety ledge running right around the pool area. The regeneration zone can also be made to slope very gently, so that children have time to notice the water becoming deeper and cannot fall in unawares. Shallow steps leading gradually into the water are easier and safer to use than a ladder. All surfaces around the pool should be made from non-slip materials, evenly laid on a stable base. Glazed tiles and polished stone should be avoided; instead, choose materials with a textured finish, such as unglazed tiles, brick or concrete. Gravelled steps, rubber mats and

Photo: Wassergarten

stones set in concrete are especially safe. Brushing the surface of newly laid concrete will create a non-slip finish. Boulders and stepping stones in the water must be made absolutely stable. The surfaces of stones should not be too smooth, so that they provide a secure grip, but you should also ensure that there are no sharp edges that could cause injury. Wooden structures such as decks, bridges and ladders should have a rippled surface so that there is no danger of slipping, even in wet or icy weather. They will also need to be scrubbed regularly to prevent any build-up of slippery algae.

Wooden structures need to be sturdily constructed so that they cannot warp or break. They should also be carefully finished so that there is no danger of splinters. A handrail is advisable on bridges and steps. Make sure that it is completely secure, bearing in mind that any children are likely to use it to swing on.

Photo: Fairwater Ltd.

Electrics

Water and electricity are a potentially dangerous combination. All electrical installations should be undertaken only by a qualified expert and must be thoroughly tested for safety before being put into use. Cables and wires must be isolated from moisture and protected from mechanical damage.

Please refer to Chapter 5 for information on the safety aspects of electrical installations in and around the pool.

Lighting

If the pool area is to be used at night, any expanses of water must be clearly lit. This is particularly important for natural pools, where lush planting could disguise deep water. If the pool itself is to be used in the evening, install lighting to illuminate the approach and the entry area. Underwater lighting will also make swimming after dark safer.

Poisonous Plants

A number of popular garden plants are toxic when touched, while others have thorns. These should be avoided around a pool where children (or adults!) will be playing.

Chemicals

Do not use pressure-treated timber for structures in and around the pool, as the chemicals used to treat the wood can leach into the water, and they may also be a danger to human health. Avoid chemicals when cleaning wooden or stone structures around the pool, as these too can damage the biological balance of the water. A thorough cleaning with water usually suffices. If necessary you can use a high-pressure cleaner, but only with water from a tested source, and without detergents.

Pathogens

Every swimmer brings germs into the pool, but these are quickly consumed by water-purifying organisms. However, one should still not swallow water from a natural swimming pool. If the pool is being used heavily, during school holidays for instance, it is advisable to increase the pump's running time to ensure that the filtration of the water is adequate. Disinfectants should never be used in a natural swimming pool, as these kill off beneficial as well as pathogenic organisms in the water.

Animals

Domestic and wild animals should be kept away from a natural pool, since they can harm the plants and the water quality. If ducks or other waterfowl settle in the pool for any length of time, their droppings can foul the water. The pool should not be used for the following three weeks, or until the water has cleared.

AQUATIC PRODUCTS

Both of the following products are useful for the natural swimming pool system.

Siltex

Siltex is a natural mineral form of ground champagne chalk which gives a number of benefits when applied to aquatic problems:

Clarifies water by flocculating fine suspended sediment and algae.

Breaks down organic silt, leaves, etc. in the pool bottom, naturally lowering silt levels (will not do so with mineral silts).

Stops the release of methane from anaerobic organic layers in the bottom of pools.

Changes the aquatic environment favourably by countering acid anaerobic conditions and raising pH.

Allows aerobic micro-organisms to breed and bread down dead organic matter.

Allows beneficial aquatic insect and plant life to develop raising oxygen levels and improving the environment for fish.

Siltex's finely ground porous chalk particles introduce aerobic bacteria and raise pH in acidic, decaying, anaerobic organic matter in pools, allowing it to break down much faster, lowering silt levels without dredging the clarified water allows sunlight to filter through bringing further beneficial changes to the aquatic environment. Siltex was discovered by accident when a pipeline trance was cut through a stream bed into chalk, and the resulting chalk sediment completely altered and improved the downstream aquatic environment. Siltex can be spread manually over the surface of the Regeneration Zone.

Zeolite – for Swimming Pool Filters

The combination of physical entrapment of fine particles and molecular sieving of contaminants makes

Zeolite (clinoptilolite) a superb water filtration medium producing superior water clarity compared to conventional sand fillers.

Absorbs ammonia, reducing the formation of chloramines and reducing the requirement for chlorine by around 30%. Chloramines are believed to be carcinogenic and have been implicated as a cause of asthma in children. Stinging eyes, skin irritation and chemical odours are greatly reduced.

Has a far greater capacity than sand, reducing the frequency of back washing by up to 50%. Regeneration can be simply achieved by soaking the zeolite overnight in a 10% salt solution.

Is a hard robust mineral. Its resistance to attrition means it will keep working year after year.

Its ability to elevate the pH of mildly acidic water reduces corrosion and rust formation.

Absorbs calcium, magnesium and iron, reducing problems of scale and staining.

GLOSSARY – Construction

Aggregate: similar to ballast, a loose mixture of crushed stone and sand used to reinforce concrete or build roads.

Armoured cabling: cabling with reinforced protective covering for safety.

Backfill: to fill in a hole around the object occupying it, for example a rigid pool unit or a plant root ball.

Ballast: a sand and gravel mix used in making concrete.

Ball valve: automatic device to control the water level of a pond or pool. A lightweight ball floats on the surface of the water. When the water level drops, a rod attached to the ball releases a valve, which allows water to flow in. As the ball rises, the rod progressively closes the valve.

Bearers: load-bearing timbers used in the construction of wooden decks, pergolas, etc.

Bedding mortar: a mixture of sand and cement used for laying paving stones.

Bentomat: a waterproof lining material containing bentonite.

Bentonite: a powder derived from fossilised volcanic ash which, when mixed with water and added to clay, swells into a water-resistant gel.

Block rock: 'as quarried' rock having roughly rectangular faces, the maximum length of side being no longer than twice the minimum.

Bubble fountain: fountain effect producing a low bubble of water forced up by a pump concealed in an underground reservoir of water.

Butyl: strong, durable, waterproof material made of rubber.

Clay puddling: a technique used for sealing and waterproofing the sides and base of large natural ponds by 'puddling', or working, the natural or added clay by hand, foot or machine.

Concrete: a mixture of sand, cement, water and small stones, which sets to form an extremely strong, durable building material; often used to make foundations.

Conduit: a tube or duct conducting water or enclosing cables.

Coping: the top course of stones or bricks in a wall; often flat or sloping stones that differ from those used in the wall, for decorative effect or to allow rainwater to run off.

Culvert: an aperture in, eg brickwork that allows water to flow out from a concealed header pool or tank.

Datum peg: a wooden peg driven into the ground; the top of, or a mark on, the peg is used as a reference point to establish a horizontal level.

Decks: areas surrounding a pool that are specifically constructed or installed for use by bathers, usually of timber.

Delivery pipe: the pipe that runs from a pump to the water outlet in a recirculating feature.

Elbow joint: a length of connecting pipe bent to form a right-angle.

Engineering brick: a dense, hard, water-resistant brick, dark in colour and hence inconspicuous under water.

Flow adjuster: an adjustable valve used to control water flow.

Footing: a narrow trench foundation, usually for a wall.

Foundation: a solid base, often of concrete, on which a structure stands.

Frictional headloss: a loss of pressure in a pipe caused by friction between the flow of liquid and the pipe itself. It is measured as the difference in head level required to overcome the headloss.

Gabions: rectangular or tubular baskets made from steel wire or polymer mesh and subsequently filled with stones.

Galvanised: of metal objects such as nails, with a coating of zinc to protect them from rusting.

Geotextile: permeable synthetic fabric used in conjunction with soil for the function of filtration, separation, drainage, soil reinforcement or erosion protection.

Gravel: a mixture of rock fragments and small pebbles that is coarser than sand.

Hardcore: broken bricks, concrete, or stones used to create a firm base for foundations or paving. Also know as ballast.

Hard protection: collective term for bank protection with materials such as steel, concrete, etc., as distinct from protection with natural 'soft' materials such as vegetation.

Hardwood: a resilient timber from deciduous trees. It is very resistant to rotting and, although expensive, is excellent for timber decking, etc.

Head: the difference in the depth of water at any two points, or the measure of the pressure at the lower point expressed in terms of this difference.

Header pool: the uppermost pool in a recirculating water feature.

Hose connector: a moulded plastic joint used to join two pipes together.

Hp - horsepower: a measure used for larger capacity pumps.

Hydraulic short-circuiting: takes place when the inlet and outlet of a tank or pond are close together and flow takes the shortest possible path allowing a large volume of the liquid to be undisturbed.

Hypertufa: a concrete mix incorporating some organic matter, encouraging mosses and algae to grow on its surface for an 'antique' effect.

JCB: a large earth-moving machine used in the excavation of ponds, pools and swimming pools.

Joist: a wooden supporting beam that runs beneath and usually perpendicular to planks, used, eg for flooring, decking or bridges.

Leat: artificial channel, the main purpose of which is to supply water to another waterway or to water-powered mills.

Low voltage transformer: a device that changes electricity to a lower and safer voltage.

Masonry bolt: an expanding rawlbolt used for very strong fixing of wood, for example, into brickwork and stonework.

Mechanical Filter: a barrier that prevents particulate matter from cycling through a pump.

Mole drain: unlined sub-surface enclosed channel made by a special tractor-pulled plough.

Non-return valve: a valve that allows water to flow in one direction only.

Non-woven fabric: geotextile fabric produced by methods other than weaving, often with a complex fibre structure having a random matrix of filaments.

Pier: a columnar support for an arch or a span of a bridge or jetty.

Pointing: filling the joints in brickwork and stonework with mortar.

Polythene film: thin sheet of plastic material, preferably black in colour. This material is often used in coffee factories and may be known as coffee sheeting. Thicker material can be obtained and is more durable.

Preformed unit: ready-made, rigid mouldings for pools and streams.

Puddled clay: traditional pond and waterway lining material, made by pounding clay and water to make a dense mass resistant to water penetration.

Pump: a machine that forces fluid through a piped system.

PVC: a strong, durable waterproof material made of vinyl chloride.

RCCB: stands for residual current circuit breaker; a cut-out device used to detect any irregularity in an electric current.

Reconstituted stone: natural stone aggregate cast in preformed shapes such as slabs or blocks.

Residual current device (RCD): often called a circuit breaker, used as a safety measure; an automatic switch halts electricity flow in the event of a short-circuit, or if the current exceeds a pre-set safe value.

Retention time: time that flowing water is retained in tanks, filters, etc. It may be calculated from the volume of tank and the rate of flow: RT = Volume of tank/Rate of flow.

Revetment: lining of wood, stone of any suitable material to prevent the walls of pits or channels collapsing in soft soil.

Sealant: a proprietary compound used to waterproof cement, timber, etc.

Sharp sand: a sand composed of hard, angular particles, used in specific mixes with cement and water for rendering walls and similar surfaces.

Shuttering: a timber frame forming a mould into which concrete is poured to create side-walls. It is sometimes known as formwork.

Softwood: a soft timber from coniferous trees, susceptible to decay.

Space tumbler: a device for determining the angle of a slope in construction,.

Spirit level: a tool for checking horizontal levels.

Stake: a straight length of timber, used to support top-heavy plants or shrubs.

Straight-edge: a straight length of timber on which to rest a spirit level.

Submersible pump: a water-recirculating pump that is housed, and runs, under water.

Sump: a pool or container into which water drains.

Surface pump: a water-recirculating pump housed and running on dry land.

Tamp: to compress firmly.

T-piece: a T-shaped connection used to join three different pipes.

Under-gravel filters: system that relies on the flow of water through a layer of gravel before being drawn from the pond and recycled.

Underlay: cushioning material laid under flexible liner as a form of protection.

Underlayer: the layer in a revetment between the armour layer and the subsoil. It may consist of a geotextile or a granular material or both.

UV filter and magnet: a combination system that prevents the build-up of minerals on which algae thrive.

Waling: horizontal beam that supports a sheet-piled retaining wall.

Wall tie: a metal strip or wire figure-eight mortared into brickwork to cross the gap between double walls, giving them more stability.

GLOSSARY – Waterscape

Acid: in gardening, a term applied to soils with a pH lower than 7.0. Most soils are of a pH from about 5.5 to 8, still a pretty big range – but pH 3 (see pH below) is really acid. Remember the smaller the pH number the more acid it is.

Acid rain: Fossil fuels can release chemicals such as sulphur when they are burnt (as petrol is in a car, or coal is in a power station). These chemicals can dissolve in atmospheric water and make rainfall unnaturally acidic. This can cause many environmental problems.

Aerated soil: an aerated soil is dry, with lots of air in the soil structure. The opposite is a wet waterlogged soil.

Aeration: the addition of oxygen to a pond to remedy stagnant water.

Air stone: a small piece of porous material, driven by an air pump, used to provide supplemental air in a water garden, pond or aquarium.

Alluvium: fine sediments deposited by floods.

Amphibious: able to live both on land and in water.

Backwash: process of cleansing filter media and/or elements by reversing water flow.

Backwash Cycle: time required to backwash filter media and/or elements and contents of the filter vessel.

Bar deposit: layer of river bed load material deposited on the inside of a bend.

Bay: recess in the water margin of a pond or lake.

Berm: shelf or ledge in the bank of a watercourse or water body.

Biofilm: accumulation of algae, bacteria and other micro-organisms on damp or wet surfaces.

Bog: mire containing acid-loving plants.

Bog garden: an area where the soil is permanently damp.

Bog plants: plants that will grow and thrive with their roots in wet soil; many will also grow in shallow water, and are more properly called marginal plants.

Calcereous: a term applied to soil containing chalk or lime.

Carr: fen scrub.

Catchment: area of ground which collects and feeds waterway or wetland.

Chalk: calcium carbonate, chemically identical to limestone. Chalk is used as a hydrated lime to counteract a high acid content in soils; a chalk soil has a high pH.

Chlorine: a chemical used to sterilize water.

Clay: a term applied to a soil mixture of very fine sand and alumina, which is moisture-retentive, heavy and sticky but usually fertile if treated.

Colloidal material: solid particles suspended in water of such a small size that they cannot be settled or filtered by simple means.

Deciduous: a term applied to a plant or tree that drops its leaves in winter.

Deep Area: Portions of a pool having water depths in excess of 1.50 metres.

Degradation: regional drop in bed level of a channel; opposite is termed aggradation.

Drain: man-made open watercourse for receiving and conveying drainage flow.

Draw-down: localised lowering of the water table around a groundwater abstraction point.

Dyke: ditch or watercourse that functions, at least in part, as a barrier; in Scotland, a dry-stone wall.

Dystrophic: water of no or extremely low productivity.

Ecology: study of how living things relate to their environment or surroundings.

Ecosystem: the totality in which any living organism finds itself.

Ecotone: area between zones which may in itself constitute a zone with its own communities.

Embankment: man-made bank to raise natural bank level in order to prevent flooding, generally constructed of soil.

Equivalent Length: A value determined by test that allows the head loss of various pipe fittings to be equated to a loss in a given length of straight pipe.

Erosion: the gradual wearing away and destruction of soil, etc, due to the effects of water or wind.

Evergreen: a plant or tree that drops and replaces its leaves gradually throughout the year, so that its branches are never bare.

Eutrophic: water of high productivity.

Eutrophication: the process where a waterbody, such as a lake, becomes loaded with dissolved phosphate nutrients. This can be natural, but is often due to pollution. Algal blooms can remove oxygen in the water harming fish life.

Evaporation: this is the rate of water loss from liquid to vapour (gaseous) state from an open water, wetted soil or plant surface.

Evapotranspiration: the rate of water loss from liquid to vapour (gaseous) state through transpiration from vegetation and evaporation from soil and plant surfaces.

Exotic: a plant not indigenous to the country in which it is growing, and which is not able to naturalize.

Fen: mire containing neutral or alkaline-loving plants.

Fetch: direct horizontal distance (in direction of the wind) over which wind generates waves.

Fill-up water: water which is added to the system from the outside, either for initial filling of the system or for topping up at a later stage (e.g. for cooling and for compensation of evaporation and water losses due to swimmers).

Filter: Device that separates solid particles from water by recirculating it through a porous substance (a filter media or element). Within the body of rules and regulations, the term 'filter' is used for devices which separate materials out from the water through biological, phsycial and/or physical-chemical methods.

> **Permanent Media Filter:** A filter that utilizes a media that can be regenerated and will not have to be replaced.

> **Diatomaceous Earth Filter:** A filter that utilizes a thin layer of diatomaceous earth as its filter media that periodically must be replaced.

> **Cartridge Filter:** A filter that utilizes a porous cartridge as its media.

Filter Cycle: Operating time between cleaning and/or backwash cycles.

Filtration Rate: Rate of filtration of water through a filter during the filter cycle expressed in US gallons per minute per square foot of effective filter area.

Filtration Zone: Filter body which is either planted or unplanted and through which the water flows in a controlled manner.

Fissured rock: rock containing many cracks which may behave as water channels.

Flash: small depression with shallow water, which may be natural or excavated.

Flocculation and coagulation: processes in which chemicals are added to water to produce a precipitate which combines with solid material suspended in the water and enables it to settle to the bottom leaving a clear top layer.

Flood meadow: pasture adjacent to a river that is regularly inundated by natural flooding.

Flood plain: flat land on either side of a river over which flood waters spread, although this may be prevented by flood protection works.

Fluvio-glacial: material transported and deposited by rivers and glaciers during the Ice Age.

Free-standing water: in the sense of this body of rules and regulations, this means water in the swimming area and in the regeneration area which is not contained in filter elements, pipes or technical equipment.

Friable: soil that crumbles easily due to a high organic content.

Fungicide: a substance used for destroying fungal diseases, usually based on copper or sulphur.

Glacial till: unsorted clays, sands, gravels and stones left by melting glaciers.

Groundwater: water stored in the pores and voids of rocks in the saturated zone below the water table.

Habit: the general appearance or manner or growth of a plant: for example, upright, weeping, creeping, etc.

Habitat: the recognisable area or type of environment in which an organism normally lives.

Half-hardy: a plant that needs protection in winter if there is a chance of frosts.

Hardpan: a virtually impermeable layer of compacted soil.

Headwater: part of a river system near to the source.

Herbaceous: a plant with a soft or sappy, instead of woody, growth.

Humus: decayed, stable organic matter found in soil and necessary for good moisture retention.

Hybrid: the product of a cross between plants of different species. It is often indicated by a cross (x) between two other plant names.

Hydrogen potential (pH): a measure of the relative acidity or alkalinity of water or soil (see pH).

Inorganic: a fertilizer or any chemical compound without carbon

Insecticide: a chemical substance used to kill harmful insects. A wide variety of products is available, either in liquid or powder form. Very selective insecticides are now commonly available and all should be used according to the accompanying instructions.

Leach: the process by which percolating water removes nutrients from the soil.

Leaf mould: the part-decayed leaves that have reached the flaky, brown stage. It looks a little like coarse peat.

Limestone: mineral consisting mainly of calcium carbonate ($CaCO_2$). It is not the same as lime, oxide of lime, quicklime or road-lime, which are all calcium oxide (CaO), or slaked lime, which is calcium hydroxide (Ca(OH)2). These other substances can be used to correct acidity but they are more soluble in water and need to be dosed in the correct proportions.

Marginal shelf: a shallow shelf built into the side of a pool where marginal plants can be stood in baskets or planted.

Marsh: area of mineral-based soil in which the summer water level is close to the surface but seldom much above it.

Mesotrophic: water of medium productivity.

Micron: one micron is 1000th or a millimetre.

Mire: area of permanently wet peat.

Montmorillonite: any of a group of clay minerals characterized by the ability to expand when they absorb large quantities of water.

Morphology: science of form and structure of, eg a river channel.

Mulch: any decayed or part-decayed organic matter that is spread around the base of plants. It is useful for preventing excessive evaporation of moisture from the soil and also helps to feed the plants. If weed suppression only is required, then inorganic material, such as gravel, can be used as a mulch.

Native: a term applied to a plant that is indigenous to a locality or country.

Natural succession: the process by which one community of organisms gives way to another in an orderly series from colonisers to climax.

Naturalize: the process of growing plants under conditions that are as nearly natural as possible. Naturalized plants are those that were originally imported but have subsequently reseeded themselves into the wild.

Non-point sources: diffuse sources of water pollution that do not emanate from single location.

Oliogotrophic: water of low productivity, low in plant nutrients.

Overall water: water from all areas of the natural pool.

Overflow System: Perimeter-type overflows, surface skimmers and surface-water collection systems of various design and manufacture.

Overflow System: surface of water established by the height of the overflow rim.

Pan: a hard, distinct soil layer caused by the precipitation of iron or other compounds.

Pathogenic organisms: organisms responsible for disease.

Peak demand: highest rate of consumption measured at any time, in practice the peak demand may last for no more than a few minutes. It may be found when all taps and other outlets in a system are operating fully open at the same time.

Pea shingle: fine gravel.

Peat: Acidic, part-decayed organic matter used as a planting medium. Moss peat comes from mainly decomposed sphagnum moss, whereas sedge peat comes from the roots and leaves of sedges.

Ped block: roughly rectangular block of material formed during break-up of bank comprising cohesive soil.

Permeable strata: layers of soil or other minerals through which water can freely drain. Impermeable strata, such as clay will retain water and prevent drainage.

Planting zone: substrate and layer which is planted and through which the water flows in a non-controlled manner.

Pool: area of deeper water within a watercourse; pond, especially within a wetland.

Precipitation: water reaching the ground from both rainfall, snow and hail.

Pure water: water which has been purified.

Recirculation rate: the frequency with which the water in the swimming area flows through the filtration zone/regeneration area within a certain period of time.

Regeneration area: the area used for biological, physical and physical/chemical urification of the water which is not accessible to swimmers.

Regenerative plants: plant types which may be suitable both for water cleansing but also for securing the waterside, soil conservation, water retention, etc.

Certain types of marsh plants (helophytes, amphiphytes) in particular and water plants which live submerged under the water (submergent and floating hydrophytes) may be suitable for the biological cleansing of water in natural pools.

Reservoir pool: a pool at the lowest point of a water feature.

Root ball: a cluster of roots embedded in soil.

Runoff: Runoff occurs as water falling as precipitation does not soak deep into the soil, but passes across the surface and near-surface towards the rivers.

Scale: the precipitate that forms on surfaces on contact with water when calcium hardness, pH or total alkalinity is too high.

Sediment: this is a deposit of 'alluvium' laid down in water (such as lakes or the sea). Sediments can, over time, form rocks such as chalk and limestone. The opposite is 'erosion'.

Seepage: movement of water into or out of the channel bank.

Shallow Areas: Portions of pool ranging in water depth from 900 to 1500 mm.

Shoal: shallow area in watercourse caused by deposition of sediment.

Shoaling: build-up of erosion material in a watercourse.

Shingle: small, rounded pebbles, sometimes used as a surface material for paths, etc.

Shrub: a multi-stemmed woody plant smaller than a tree.

Silt: that mineral fraction of the soil with particles from 0.002-0.063mm diameter

fine silt: 0.002-0.006mm diameter

medium silt: 0.006-0.02mm diameter

coarse silt: 0.02-0.063mm diameter

Single-area system: the areas of the pool intended for swimming and regeneration area are located within a single basin/pool.

Skimmer System: surface of the water that should be kept at the mid-point of the operating range of a skimmer.

Softwood timber: timber cut from coniferous trees.

Species: a group of plants that resemble each other, breed together and maintain the same constant distinctive character.

Specimen plant: a tree or shrub grown so that it is prominent and can be seen from many different angles.

Stagnant: water that is stale and sluggish, usually lacking in oxygen.

Subsoil: the soil within the bank of a channel, or behind the bank protection, beneath topsoil.

Substrate: An inclusive term for the soil used when describing, for instance, the portion in which plant roots exist.

Supplementary area: areas which do not immediately belong to the natural swimming pool but are added for its use, e.g. paths and access routes to the pool, rest areas and areas for lying down, playing areas for children.

Swimming area: the area designated for swimming in. This includes e.g. areas for swimmers and non-swimmers.

Swimming and natural pool: pool system designed especially for swimming. It is sealed against the subsoil and comprises the swimming area and the regeneration area, and it has defined requirements in terms of water quality. The water is cleansed biologically, in addition possibly also physically or physically/chemically; referred to in the following as "natural pool".

TDS: Total dissolved solids; the sum total of all dissolved material in the water.

Topsoil: the top layer of soil, which contains plant nutrients.

Total Alkalinity: the measure of alkaline components present in pool water. These components act as a buffering agent against rapid pH changes.

Turbidity: Cloudy condition of water due to the presence of extremely fine particulate materials in suspension.

Two-area or multiple-area system: the swimming area(s) and regeneration area(s) are separated by structural means.

Ultraviolet (UV) light: ultraviolet is a high energy, short wavelength of light, shorter than violet in the visible spectrum and on the border of the x-ray region.

Untreated water: water from the swimming area which is conveyed to the regeneration area.

Variety: a group of plants within a species; any plant with distinctive characteristics but not worthy of a specific rank.

Washland: area of frequently flooded flat land adjacent to a river.

Water circulation: the quantity of water moved as a result of addition and removal between the swimming area and the regeneration area and possible the water reservoir.

Watercourse: natural or man-made channel that conveys water.

Waterline: defined in one of the following ways:

Water meadow: a frequently flooded, low-lying area of ground usually comprising rough grass and supporting a variety of wild plants and flowers.

Water purification: procedure which ensures that the requirements in terms of a suitable water quality are satisfied.

Water table: the level under the ground to which water naturally drains. This varies from locality to locality depending on the composition of the underlying rock.

Waterway: channel used for navigation.

Weir: a dam built across a stream or river designed to raise the water level upstream.

Wick effect: tendency of water to move from a pond to surrounding soil, drawn by the plant's root system.

Photo: Haderstorfer Garten – Landschafts und Sportplatzbau

GLOSSARY – Biological

Acidic: with a pH level of less than 7 (see pH)

Aerobic: characterised by the presence of free or molecular oxygen; requiring such conditions to live.

Aeromonas bacteria: a genus of gram-negative, facultatively anaerobic bacteria. Its organisms are found in fresh water and sewage and are pathogenic to humans, frogs and fish.

Alga: (plural: algae) Simple plants ranging from single cells (unicellular algae) to larger ones visible to the naked eye. These in include the filamentous algae e.g blanket-weed or cott and the stoneworts.

Algae: Simple unicellular organisms, which cause pool and pond water to look green. These organisms multiply rapidly in conditions of high temperature and high natural light levels.

Algal growth: growth of very small water plants which may help to reduce pollution in water but if they become too numerous cause difficulties in water treatment such as clogging filters, etc.

Alkaline: with a pH value above 7 (see pH), normally with a comparatively high lime content.

Alternate: leaves arising singly from the stem (see opposite).

Ammonia: (NH3) the most toxic of the nitrogen containing pollutants. Most ammonia enters the water when excreted from the fishes' gills; it is broken down into nitrate by nitrosomonas bacteria

Anaerobic: action which occurs out of contact with air or oxygen.

Anion: a negatively charged ion. The most commonly found anions in soil waters include bicarbonates, sulphates, carbonates, chlorides and nitrates.

Annual: a plant that germinates, grows, flowers, seeds and dies within the space of 12 months.

Aquatic: term applied to a plant of any genera capable of living with its roots, stems and sometimes its leaves submerged in water.

Aquatic Plant: any plant that can grow with its roots surrounded by water, either free floating or in saturated soil.

Autotrophic (bacteria): Autotrophic bacteria can take carbon in from the atmosphere through the fixation, reduction and incorporation of carbon dioxide.

Bacteria: ubiquitous one-celled organisms, various species of which are involved in fermentation, putrefaction, infectious diseases or nitrogen fixation.

Bacterial Count: a method of estimating the number of bacteria present per unit volume of water.

Biennial: a plant that germinates, grows, flowers, seeds and dies within a period of two years.

Bilharzia: a disease caused by a very small free-swimming parasite.

Bilharzia cercaria: the stage of the Bilharzia parasite when it is infective to humans. Infection is by penetration of the skin.

Bio-film: a thin layer of micro-organisms that forms on and coats various surfaces that are regularly in contact with water.

Biological filtration: a method of filtration using bacteria to change toxic compounds (eg ammonia) into safer compounds (eg nitrates).

Bladder: a small hollow sac on stems and leaves.

Blanket bog: extensive area of acid mire found on flat and gently sloping ground where rainfall is high.

Blanket weed: fibrous algae that look like long strands or filaments (sometimes called String Algae). Thick floating mats of the algae can form on ponds and deprive wildlife of oxygen.

Bog: damp areas of poorly drained ground resembling bog conditions and planted with bog and marginal plants.

Bog garden: area of poorly drained ground resembling bog conditions and planted with bog and marginal plants.

Bog plants: plants that will tolerate the continually wet conditions found in a bog.

Bract: a small leaf like structure. Bracts are usually situated at the base of a flower.

Bryophyte: a plant belonging to the Bryophyta, the group of plants which contains mosses and liverworts.

Bur: a round fruit with spines or hooks.

Channelled: with a groove or grooves running the length of a stem or leaf.

Compound leaf: a leaf made up of several distinct leaflets.

Community: group of plants and/or animals living together under characteristic, recognisable conditions.

Cordate: a leaf with two rounded lobes at its base.

Corm: a storage organ comprising a thickened underground stem.

Cross-section: view of a part of a plant, eg stem or leaf, after it has been cut across.

Cross Walls: internal walls, sometimes called ribs or interruptions which divide hollow leaves and stems into separate compartments.

Crown: the top of the rootstock from which new shoots grow.

Crucifer: a plant belonging to the family Cruciferae. These include the water-cresses.

Cultivar: Cultivated variety either bred purposely or developing spontaneously, but incapable of exact reproductions by seeds.

Dicotyledon: one of two major divisions of the flowering plants whose characteristics include diverging leaf veins (see Monocotyledons).

Dormant: a condition of inactivity in plants usually occasioned by low temperatures.

Drainage channels: artificial channels which take away drainage from the surrounding areas of ground or land. The term includes dyke, ditch and drain.

Emergent plant: a plant with erect leaves and stems which grow up out of water.

Entire: a description of a leaf margin which does not have lobes or teeth.

Facultative: having the capacity to live under more than one specific set of environmental conditions, eg a plant that can lead either a parasitic or a nonparasitic life or a bacterium that can live with or without air.

Family: a group of gene

Flaccid: limp.

Floating Plant: a plant with leaves or fronds which float on the surface of the water.

Frond: the 'leaf' of a fern.

Flamentous: resembling fine threads.

Genus: (plural genera) a group of species with certain common characteristics. Any one group carries the same scientific name, eg Lemna. Some genera contain only one species.

Habitat: the place in which a plant grows.

Hp-horsepower: a measure used for larger capacity pumps.

Hydrosoil: the 'soil' at the bottom of a waterbody – may be stony, gravely or muddy.

Larva: the growth stage of some animals between egg and adult.

Leaflet: one of a number of small leaves making up a compound leaf.

Ligule: a thin membrane sheath at the base of the leaf found only in the grasses.

Longitudinal: lengthways.

Macronutrients: these are nutrients which are needed in large quantities by plants – such as calcium, magnesium and potassium.

Macrophyte: broad leaved plant.

Marginal Plant: a plant which grows at the waters edge.

Micronutrients: these are nutrients which plants need only in small (or 'trace') amounts – such as iron, zinc, copper and boron.

Midrib: (or midvein) the conspicuous central vein of a leaf.

Mineralization: mineralization is the conversion of 'bound' organic nitrogen into the mineral (ionic or inorganic) form required for plant uptake. The inorganic nitrogen is then converted in a process known as nitrification from ammonium salts to nitrites, and from nitrites to nitrates by nitrifying bacteria which obtain their energy from this oxidation process. Once free nitrate is formed, the rapid recycling process offers many options, the nitrate may be assimilated by plants, denitrified or leached.

Moisture lovers: plants that thrive in moist soil. Unlike bog plants, moisture-lovers need some soil drainage and do not tolerate waterlogged conditions.

Monocotyledon: one of two major divisions of the flowering plant whose characteristics include parallel leaf veins (see Dicotyledon).

Nitrate: the univalent radical NO3 or a compound containing it, such as a salt or an ester of nitrous acid.

Nitrification: nitrification is the process in which the nitrogen cycle works. Ammonia is created by urea and decomposition. Ammonia is turned into nitrites by nitrosomonas bacteria. Nitrites are then converted to nitrates by nitrobacter. Nitrates are used as an agricultural fertiliser. Applied incorrectly, nitrates can pose a pollution risk.

Nitrite: the univalent radical NO$_2$ or a compound containing it, such as a salt or an ester of nitrous acid.

Nitrobacter: genus or bacteria which oxidises nitrite into nitrate.

Nitrogen cycle: the natural cycle within the pond, converting ammonia to nitrate, which is then converted to nitrate by bacterial activity.

Nitrosomonas: genus of nitrifying bacteria found in biological filtration which oxidises ammonia into nitrite.

Nutrients: nutrients are 'minerals' needed by plants and animals function and to remain healthy. Iron, calcium, potassium and sodium are minerals.

Opposite: leaves arising from the stem in pairs (see Alternate).

Oxidation: Oxidation is the addition of oxygen, removal of hydrogen or the removal of electrons from an element or compound. In the environment, organic matter is oxidized to more stable substances. Oxidation is the opposite of 'reduction'.

Oxygenator: submerged aquatic plant which performs a key functional role in ponds; the leaves and stems release oxygen into the water as a by-product of photosynthesis.

Palmate: a leaf shaped like a hand.

Panicle: a flower cluster of several separate branches, each carrying numerous stalked flowers.

Pathogen: any disease-producing agent (especially a virus or bacterium or other microorganism).

Peltate: a shield-shaped leaf with a central stalk.

Perennial: any plant that lives and flowers for a number of years.

pH: quantitative expression denoting the acidity or alkalinity of a solution or soil. It has a scale of 0 to 14; pH7 is neutral, below 7 is acid and above 7 is alkaline.

Photosynthesis: this is the important process in plant cells in which the sun's energy is used to join carbon dioxide and water to make sugar – the food of green plants.

Pinnate: a term applied to a feather-like leaf having several leaflets on each side of a common stalk.

Pith: the spongy tissue of a stem.

Pollard: tree that has been cut 2-4 metres above ground level and then allowed to regrow.

Pond: the smallest type of waterbody.

Pondweeds: the species belonging to the genus Potomogeton, or a general term for water plants.

Pool: a waterbody of a size which lies between a pond and a lake.

Raceme: an unbranched inflorescence with flowers carried on equal-length stalks.

Rank: a row of leaves, 2-,3-ranked, having the leaves in 2 or 3 distinct vertical veins.

Respiration: process in which plants and animals derive energy by means of internal chemical reactions, generally using oxygen and giving out carbon dioxide.

Rhizome: an underground stem that usually grows horizontally, producing shoots some distance from the parent.

Rosette: a group of leaves originating from a common point of attachment.

Runner: an above ground creeping stem from which shoots arise.

Saggitate: an arrow-shaped leaf with two lobes projecting backwards, giving it the appearance of an arrow head.

Sluggish: slow moving.

Soda Ash: Also called sodium carbonate, it is a white powder used to raise pH in water.

Sodium Bicarbonate: Baking soda, a white powder used to raise total alkalinity in water.

Sodium Bisulphate: Dry acid, used to lower pH and total alkalinity.

Species: the smallest unit used to classify plants and animals. A species belong to a particular genus eg Lemna minor.

Spike: a sharply pointed stem or in the case of a flower-spike, a group of flowers arranged on the stem in the shape of a spike.

Spore-bearing cone: the part of a plant which produces the spores.

Stonewort: a plant belonging to a genus such as Chara or Nitella. These are algae but resemble certain types of higher plants.

String Algae: see 'blanket weed'.

Submerged plants: plants that for the most part, have totally submerged foliage and, in many cases, emergent flowers.

Succession: replacement of one type of community by another, shown by progressive changes in vegetation and animal life.

Swamp: area of mineral soil normally flooded in the growing season and dominated in most cases by emergent macrophytes.

Taproot: a straight root, thicker at its top than at its bottom, from which subsidiary roots grow.

Terminal: occurring at the end of stems, leaves, etc.

Toothed: an irregular leaf edge.

Translucent: permitting light to pass through but not entirely transparent.

Trifoliate: comprising three leaflets in a clover shape.

Tubular: cylindrical and hollow.

Umbel: an umbrella-shaped cluster of flowers.

Umbellifer: a plant of the family Umbelliferae which includes the water-dropworts.

Under-gravel filters: system that relies on the flow of water through a layer of gravel before being drawn from the pond and recycled.

Unicellular: consisting of a single cell.

Virus: a non-cellular infectious agent that reproduces only in living cells.

Whorl: three or more leaves originating from the stem at the same level.

Zeolite: a type of ion exchange media use for removing ammonia from pond or water garden water.

Zonation: the occurrence of communities in distinct geographical areas or zones.

Zooplankton: animals occurring in the water which are often microscopic in size.

ORGANISATIONS

UNITED KINGDOM

British Association of Natural Swimming Pools
c/o Unit 105, Screen Works, 22 Highberry Grove,
London N5 2EF
Tel: 020 7183 3333
Email: info@bansp.org
Web: www.bansp.org

Landscape Institute
33 Great Portland Street, London W1 8QG
Tel: 0207 299 4500
Fax: 0207 299 4501
Email: mail@landscapeinstitute.org
Web: www.landscapeinstitute.org

Society of Garden Designers
Katepwa House, Ashfield Park Avenue,
Ross on Wye, Herefordshire HR9 5AX
Tel: 01989 566695
Fax: 01989 567676
Email: info@sgd.org.uk
Web: www.sgd.org.uk

Association of Professional Landscapers
Horticulture House, 19 High Street,
Theale, Reading, Berks RG7 5AH
Tel: 0118 930 3132
Email: hta@martex.co.uk
Web: www.martex.co.uk/hta

British Association of Landscape Industries
Landscape House, Stoneleigh Park,
Warwickshire CV8 2LG
Tel: 024 7669 0333
Email: info@bali.co.uk
Web: www.bali.co.uk

Centre for Ecology and Hydrology
CEH Wallingford, Maclean Building,
Crowmarsh Gifford, Wallingford, Oxon OX10 8BB
Tel: 01491 838800
Email: enquiries@ceh.ac.uk
Web: www.ceh.ac.uk

EUROPE

International Body for Natural Bathing Water
Aichbergstrasse 48, A-4600 Wels, Austria

USA

American Society of Landscape Architects
636 Eye Street, NW Washington, DC 20001-3736
Tel: 202 898 2444
Fax: 202 898 1185
Web: www.asla.org

National Association of Pond Professionals
PO Box 369, Epworth, GA 30541
Tel: 706 258 3534
Fax: 706 632 0300
Web: www.nationalpondpro.com

AUSTRALIA

NZ Institute of Landscape Architects
PO Box 10 022, The Terrace, Wellington
Email: info@nzila.co.nz

Landscape Industries Association of NZ
PO Box 5523, Auckland
Email: admin@lianz.org.nz
Web: www.lianz.org.nz

NEW ZEALAND

NZ Institute of Landscape Architects
POBox 10 022
The Terrace
Wellington
Email: info @nzila.co.nz

Landscape Industries Association of NZ
PO Box 5523
Auckland

www.lianz.org.nz
Email: admin@lianz.org.nz

CANADA

Canadian Society of Landscape Architects
PO Box 13594, Ottawa, ONK2 K1X6

RESEARCH

REFERENCES

Dobler, Anna and Wolfgang Fleischer. *Schwimmteiche*. ORAC, Austria, 1999.

Dreiseitl, Dieter Grau and Karl H.C. Ludwig. *Waterscapes - Planning, Building and Designing with Water*. Birkhauser, Basel, Berlin, Boston, 2001.

English Nature. *Water Level Requirements of selected plants and animals, 1997*.

Franke, Wolfram. *der Traum vom eigenen Schwimmteich*. BLV, 2001

Leopold Stocker Verlag, 2003

Littlewood, Michael. *Landscape Detailing* 1 *Enclosure,* Architectural Press, Oxford, 1993.

Littlewood, Michael. *Landscape Detailing* 2 *Surfaces,* Architectural Press, Oxford, 1993.

Littlewood, Michael. *Landscape Detailing* 3 *Structures,* Architectural Press, Oxford, 1997.

Littlewood, Michael. *Landscape Detailing* 4 *Water,* Architectural Press, Oxford, 2001.

Matson, Tim. *Earth Ponds: The country pond maker's guide to building, maintenance and restoration,* 2nd ed., revised and expanded. Woodstock, Vermont, USA: Countryman Press, 1991.

Robinson, Peter. *Water Gardening.* Royal Horticultural Society and Dorling Kindersley, 1997.

Seyerle, Guido. *Der Weg zum eigenen Schwimmteich.* AgriMedia GmbH, 2005

Stein, Siegfried. *Bachläufe und Badeteiche Selber Bauen.* Munich: Callwey,

Weixler, Richard and Wolfgang Hauer. *Garten und Schwimmteiche.*

Weixler, Richard. *Freude mit dem eigenen Schwimmteich.* AgriMedia GmbH, 2007

BIBLIOGRAPHY

Archer-Willis, Anthony. *The Water Gardener.* Frances Lincoln, 1993.

Champion, Chrystal A. *Natural Swimming Pools.* Pennsylvania, USA: Dissertation, 2003.

Chinery, Michael. *The Living Garden.* Dorling Kindersley, 1986.

Dawes, John. *The Pond Owners' Handbook.* Ward Lock, 1998.

Erler, Catriona Tudor. *Pool Scaping*, Storey Books, USA 2003

Paul, Anthony and Yvonne Rees. *The water garden: a complete illustrated guide to creating and planting pools and water features.* Guild Publishing, 1986.

Roberts, Debbie and Ian Smith. *Creating Garden Ponds and Water Feature.* London: Harper Collins, 2001.

Timm, Ulrich. *Creating Ponds, Brooks & Pools.* Atglen, Pennsylvania: Schiffer Publishing Ltd., 2001.

Timm, Ulrich. *Die Neuen Teiche, Bache, Pools.* Munich: Callwey.

ACKNOWLEDGEMENTS

I would like to express my sincere appreciation to the many people who have assisted me with this book and the previous title A Guide for Building, *as without their support it would not have been published.*

Manuscript/Technical Information

CLIENTS
Simon Allen
John Fulton
David Hartgill
Tim Rickard

CONTRACTORS
Steve Day, Anglo Swimming Ponds
Tim Evans, Garten Art
Martin Kelley, Fairwater Ltd
Will Woodhouse, Woodhouse Natural Pools Ltd

Technical Information

Tony Harragin for checking all the construction and technical data
Martin Kelley for allowing use of his own DIY manual, including technical drawings

Drawings

Peter Thomas	Computer Aided Draughting
Neil Reed	Sketch

Photographs/Images

David Hartgill	
Stefan Lehnert	Lehnert Erb AG, Switzerland
Richard Weixler	Wassergarten, Austria
Rosalind Everett	Anglo Swimming Ponds
Martin Kelley	Fairwater Ltd
Will Woodhouse	Woodhouse Natural Pools Ltd

Graphics

Andrew Crane

Word Processing

Kat Kahn-Davis

Technical Advisors

John Dawes, Fellow of Institute of Pool Engineers

Production

Andrew Crane for his wonderful and practical layout, typography, and graphics. A superb job.

Gaby Bartai for editing the new text for this edition.

Peter Thomas for converting my sketches into the usual high-standard technical drawings.

Ian Robertson of Schiffer Publishing for his considerable assistance and tenacity.

Pete Schiffer of Schiffer Publishing for publishing my book.

MEASUREMENTS

METRIC/IMPERIAL CONVERSION

	Metric	Imperial
LENGTH	1 millimetre (mm)	0.0394 in
	1 centimetre (cm) / 10mm	0.3937 in
	1 metre / 100cm	39.37 in / 3.281 ft / 1.094 yd
	1 kilometre (km) 1000 metres	1093.6 yd / 0.6214 mile
	25.4mm / 2.54cm	1 inch
	304.8mm / 30.48cm / 0.3048m	1 foot (ft) 12in
	914.4mm / 91.44cm / 0.9144m	1 yard (yd) 3ft
	1609.344 metres / 1.609km	1 mile / 1760 yd
AREA	1 square centimetre(sq cm) / 100 square millimetres(sq mm)	0.155 sq in
	1 square metre(sq metre) / 10,000sq cm	10.764 sq ft / 1.196 sq yd
	1 are / 100 sq metres	119.60 sq yd / 0.0247 acre
	1 hectare (ha) / 100 ares	2.471 acres / 0.00386 sq mile
	645.16 sq mm / 6.4516 sq cm	1 square inch(sq in)
	929.03 sq cm	1 square foot(sq ft) 144sq in
	8361.3 sq cm / 0.8361 sq m	1 square yard(sq yd) / 9 sq ft
	4046.9 sq m / 0.4047 ha	1 acre / 4840 sq yd
	259 ha / 2.59 sq km	1 square mile / 640 acres
VOLUME	1 cubic centimetre (cu cm) / 10000 cubic centimetres (cu mm)	0.0610 cu in
	1 cubic decimetre (cu dm) / 1000 cu cm	61.024 cu in / 0.0353 cu ft
	1 cubic metre / 1000 cu dm	35.3147 cu ft / 1.308 cu yd
	1 cu cm = 1 millilitre (ml)	
	1 cu dm = 1 litre (see Capacity)	
	16.3871 cu cm	1 cubic inch (cu in)
	28,316.8 cu cm / 0.0283 cu metre	1 cubic foot (cu ft) / 1728 cu in
	0.7646 cu metre	1 cubic yard (cu yd) / 27 cu ft

	Metric	Imperial
	1 litre	1.7598 pt / 0.8799 qt / 0.22 gal
CAPACITY	0.568 litre	1 pint (pt)
	1.137 litres	1 quart (qt)
	4.546 litres	1 gallon (gal)
	1 gram(g)	0.035 oz
	1 kilogram (kg) / 1000 g	2.20 lb / 35.2 oz
	1 tonne / 1000 kg	2204.6 lb / 0.9842 ton
WEIGHT	28.35 g	1 ounce (oz)
	0.4536 kg	1 pound (lb)
	1016 kg	1 ton
	1 gram per square metre (g / metre^2)	0.0295 oz / sq yd
	1 gram per square centimetre (g / cm^2)	0.228 oz / sq in
	1 kilogram per square centimetre (kg / cm^2)	14.223 lb / sq in
	1 kilogram per square metre (kg / metre^2)	0.205 lb / sq ft
PRESSURE	4.882 kg / metre^2	1 pound per square foot (lb / ft^2)
	703.07 kg / metre^2	1 pound per square inch (lb / in^2)
	305.91 g / metre^2	1 ounce per square yard (oz / yd^2)
	305.15 g / metre^2	1 ounce per square foot (oz / ft^2)
TEMPERATURE	To convert °F to °C, subtract 32, then divide by 9 and multiply by 5	
	To convert °C to °F, divide by 5 and multiply by 9, then add 32	
STRESS	1 N / mm^2	147 lbs / sq inch
	15.2 N / mm^2	1 ton / sq inch
	1 KN / m^2	0.009 tons / sq ft
	107 KN / m^2	1 ton / sq ft
	1 KN / m	68.5 lbs / ft

CONCLUSION

Building your own pool is an immensely rewarding project. I hope that this book has inspired you to undertake your own natural swimming pool project, and that it will enable you to achieve results of which you can be rightly proud.

Recent DIY natural swimming pool projects have come in at around 35 to 50 per cent of the cost of a professional installation, and that alone makes the self-build route worth exploring, as the reduced cost brings the benefits and pleasures of a natural pool within reach for many more people. Even more important to self-builders is the sense of fulfilment and achievement they feel at having created something so inspirational.

David Butler, who built a pool in his garden in Norfolk, England, says, 'Building my own natural swimming pool has been my most rewarding experiment. Three years in the making, the ecosystem is stabilising and the water is sparkling clear... And those couple of years of hard work ripple away with every splash of a bathing swallow, and each sight of a kingfisher hunting for water beetles. And, of course, there is the joy of swimming in soft rainwater!'

The message from this and the many other successful self-build projects is clear: take the plunge!

Photo: Woodhouse Natural Pools Ltd.

THE AUTHOR

Michael Littlewood is a natural landscape architect and environmental planner with extensive experience of designing and implementing sustainable land use projects. His mission has been the introduction of ecological design and planning into the mainstream.

His reputation derives from work over many years in the UK, Australia, New Zealand, Saudi Arabia, Malaysia, Greece and Portugal, in a wide variety of situations, landscapes and climates. His clients have included national, regional and local governments, universities, colleges and schools, landowners and developers, and the owners of farms, estates and gardens.

His designs incorporate his specialisms of eco-building, bio-engineering, renewable energy systems, waste treatments, water harvesting, natural swimming pools, organic food production, and wildlife and nature conservation. This enables him to give his clients not just the landscape amenities they require for the present but also an improved environment for the future.

Michael introduced natural swimming pools to the UK in 2000 and has been involved in the planning and design of over 50 successful projects to date. His four books on natural swimming pools have been highly commended by reviewers in Britain and the USA.

He is also the author of a number of other publications, including a series of technical books on landscape detailing, covering all aspects of construction. He has produced a range of books, posters and calendars on organic gardening and a series of brochures covering his concepts of the sustainable village, farm, school and residence.

Michael also has extensive teaching experience at universities and colleges in the UK and abroad.

In his work Michael has been guided by a belief in the necessity and value of working in harmony with nature, to a philosophy and design approach rooted in the permaculture ethics of integrating earth care with people care to the increased benefit of both. He sees his concepts as a dramatic and conspicuous example of the value of ecological design, where separating and combining functions and uses makes the most of both worlds, the natural and the artificial, while at the same time creating beauty.

Visit **www.ecodesignscape.co.uk** for full details of his design services and publications.

INDEX